ایران فارسی امروز

دوره مقدماتی آموزش زبان فارسی

آنوشا شهسواری
بلیک آتوود

جلد ۱

PERSIAN OF IRAN TODAY

AN INTRODUCTORY COURSE

VOLUME 1

ANOUSHA SHAHSAVARI | BLAKE ATWOOD

CENTER FOR MIDDLE EASTERN STUDIES
THE UNIVERSITY OF TEXAS AT AUSTIN

This project would not have been possible without the generous support of the PARSA Community Foundation, the Department of Middle Eastern Studies and the Center for Middle Eastern Studies at the University of Texas at Austin and the encouragement and support of Kamran Aghaie, Kristen Brustad, Bavand Behpoor, and Chris Adams. We are especially grateful to our Iranian friends who agreed to be on film and in pictures and lent their voices to this project. Their presence made this book come alive!

Many thanks to the following people who contributed to the textbook in immeasurable ways:

The University of Texas at Austin Graduate Students: Steve Robertson, Kevin Burnham, Dena Afrasiabi, Christine Anderson, Mardin Aminpour, Hamenaz Tofangdar

Art Director and Photography: Rosa Shahsavari
Layout and Graphic Design: Reza Abedi
Videos: Mehdi Zarei, Scott Zuniga
Actors: Shyli Yazdani, Negar Kherad
Cultural Notes: Nassim Abdi
Illustrations: Gholam Ahmadi
Production and Cover Design: Kristi Shuey
Cover Art: © Faegheh Shirazi
Website Design and Maintenance: LAITS

ISBN: 978-0-578-13002-6

© 2015 The University of Texas at Austin Center for Middle Eastern Studies and Shahsavari-Atwood. All rights reserved. No part of this book may be reproduced or utilized in any form or by any means, electronic or mechanical, including photocopying and recording, or by any information storage and retrieval system, without permission in writing from the publisher.

This work is licensed under the Creative Commons Attribution-Noncommercial-No Derivative Works 3.0 United States License. To view a copy of this license, visit http://creativecommons.org/licenses/by-nc-nd/3.0/us/ or send a letter to Creative Commons, 171 Second Street, Suite 300, San Francisco, California, 94105, USA.

TABLE OF CONTENTS

To the Student vii
Tips for Using this Book viii
To the Instructor ix
Introduction to the Persian Alphabet xi
Notes on the Pronunciation of Persian xiv
Introductory Exercise xvi

Unit 1: Cultural Note: Greetings 1 2
    Short Conversations: Hello, how are you?/ What is your name?
    Alphabet: *alef*, be, nun, zebar, zir, pish, pe, te, ye, vaav
    Vocabulary: List 1
    Listening Comprehension: Greetings and Numbers
    Grammar: A Note on Names, Derivation, Word Stress, Syllable Structure

Unit 2: Cultural Note: Greetings 2 23
    Short Conversations: Thank you!
    Alphabet: dâl, re, ze, sin, shin, mim, e, he
    Vocabulary: List 1
    Listening Comprehension: Greetings, What do I like?
    Grammar: Sentence Structure or Word Order, Subject Pronouns, Verb Endings
    Writing Exercise
    Speaking Activity

Unit 3: Cultural Note: Introductions 48
    Short Conversations: I am Asadi!
    Alphabet: jim, lâm, he
    Vocabulary: List 1
    Listening Comprehension: Introduction and Asking Questions, About My Brother
    Grammar: The Verb "to be", Negating the Verb "to be"
    Writing Exercise
    Speaking Activity

Unit 4: Cultural Note: Food 63
    Short Conversations: What would you like to drink/eat?
    Alphabet: che, khe, zhe, khâ
    Vocabulary: List 1
    Listening Comprehension: What do I eat for Breakfast, Every Day conversation
    Grammar: Possession, âyâ
    Writing Exercise
    Speaking Activity

Unit 5: Cultural Note: Diverse Iran 79
    Short Conversations: Where are you from?
    Alphabet: fe, qâf, kâf, gâf
    Vocabulary: List 1, List 2: Numbers, List 3: English words in Persian
    Listening Comprehension: I Have a Class Today, Where Is Eram Hotel?, I am Sulmaz
    Grammar: Using Pronouns, Present Tense Conjugation, Counting
    Writing Exercise
    Listening Comprehension: I Have a Class Today, Where Is Eram Hotel?, I am Sulmaz

    Grammar: Using Pronouns, Present Tense Conjugation, Counting
    Writing Exercise
    Speaking Activity
    Language Game

Unit 6: Cultural Note: Hospitability **101**
    Short Conversations: Who Is This?
    Alphabet: tashdid, sâd, zâl, eyn
    Vocabulary: List 1, List 2: Home
    Listening Comprehension: My House
    Grammar: Ezâfe
    Writing Exercise
    Speaking Activity

Unit 7: Cultural Note: I Do Not Want to Bother You! **120**
    Short Conversations: How Old Are You?
    Alphabet: se, he, zâd, tâ
    Vocabulary: List 1, List 2: Numbers
    Listening Comprehension: My Plan for Tonight, Every Day Conversation
    Grammar: More on The Verb "to be", Simple and Compound Verbs
    Writing Exercise
    Speaking Activity
    Language Game

Unit 8: Cultural Note: Early Bird **140**
    Short Conversations: Good Morning!
    Alphabet: fe, qâf, kâf, gâf
    Vocabulary: List 1, List 2: Numbers
    Listening Comprehension: This Is My Friend, It Is Hot Today, Wrong Number!, What Time Is It?
    Grammar: Answering "yes" To A Negative Question
    Writing Exercise
    Speaking Activity
    Language Game

Unit 9: Cultural Note: Befarmâ'id **152**
    Short Conversations: What Do You Do?
    Alphabet: tanvin, hamze, Sokun
    Vocabulary: List 1, List 2: prepostions
    Listening Comprehension: What Do You Do and Where Do You Live?, It Was Fun!
    Grammar: Possessive Pronouns, Counting, Asking How Many, Answeing How Many, There Is
    Writing Exercise
    Speaking Activity
    Language Game: Hoarders

Unit 10: Cultural Note: Studying in Iran **166**
    Short Conversations: What Is Your Major?
    Vocabulary: List 1, List 2: Countries
    Listening Comprehension: Practice!, I Am Going to My Setâr Class Today!
    Grammar: Plural, Specific Direct Object Marker "râ"
    Speaking Activity
    Language Game

Review Exercises, Texts of Short Conversations for Units 1 & 2, and Vocabulary List 180

TO THE STUDENT

Khosh Amadid! Welcome to Persian! This textbook, *Persian of Iran Today 1*, represents the first in a series of textbooks aimed at teaching Persian to English-speaking students, and is followed by *Persian of Iran Today, Book II*.

The present book aims to help you learn to pronounce the sounds of Persian and write its letters, and to begin speaking Persian. The materials will introduce basic vocabulary, including important expressions for polite interaction and aspects of Persian culture. The book is accompanied by audio and video clips on a website for you to use outside of class. The website (http://www.laits.utexas.edu/persian_teaching_resources/) includes videos that demonstrate how to write the letters so that you have a model to follow as you work through the book.

This book consists of an introduction and ten writing units. The introduction provides an overview of Persian and introduces the Persian writing system and sounds. The ten units present the alphabet in groups following an order designed to maximize your exposure to the Persian script from the beginning, meaning that transliteration will generally be avoided. Each sound that is introduced will be followed by a brief explanation of the writing of the corresponding letter, and video footage on the website will show how to write each of the letters. Each unit contains a number of recorded listening exercises and drills on reading, writing, connecting letters, and dictation. We have used only meaningful words in these exercises, but we do not expect you to learn these words; their purpose is merely to demonstrate sounds and stress. The vocabulary that you are expected to learn is listed in a section called vocabulary.

We have also included in this book examples of authentic or "real-life" Persian from websites, newspapers, books, and magazines, and on the website you will find pictures of Persian signs from the streets of Iran. We have also included short cultural notes explaining some aspects of the situations that you will see in the clips.

We believe that it is crucial for you to learn to recognize and produce Persian sounds accurately and master the Persian script from the outset for several reasons. First, you must learn to pronounce and write Persian correctly in order to communicate effectively with Persian speakers. Second, Persian sounds are not very difficult. Many non-native speakers have learned to pronounce Persian sounds accurately, and there is no reason why you should not expect to do so as well. Third, it is important to learn the sounds and writing system correctly now when you have the time to concentrate on them; later you will be concentrating on other aspects of the language, such as vocabulary and grammar. Finally, although all languages require a certain amount of exposure, time, and effort to learn, by mastering the Persian sounds and script from the outset, you will enhance your ability to learn the language and make your future interaction with the language more rewarding.

رهنمودهایی برای استفاده از کتاب

۱.

برای مشارکت فعال در کلاس آماده باشید. برای رسیدن به این هدف، باید پیش از کلاس به فایل‌های صوتی گوش کنید، ویدیوها را ببینید و تمرین‌های آن‌ها را انجام دهید. به صداهای جدید گوش کنید و حروف جدید را بنویسید. هر چه‌قدر لازم است این کار را تکرار کنید، تا وقتی که شناختن و تولید این صداها و حروف برایتان راحت و آسان شود. تمرین‌های در خانه را پیش از کلاس انجام دهید تا برای خواندن و نوشتن در کلاس آماده باشید. وقت کلاس باید صرف تمرین شود، نه شنیدن سخنرانی استادتان.

To access online resources: http://www.laits.utexas.edu/persian_teaching_resources/

۲.

یک بار کافی نیست. هر تمرینی انجام می‌دهید، چه تمرین تلفظ صداهای جدید باشد، چه تمرین نوشتن حروف جدید و چه مطالعه و یادگیری واژه‌ها، باید هر چند بار که ممکن است، تکرار شود. تا آنجا تکرار کنید که تلفظ صداها و نوشتن حروف برای‌تان راحت شود. توجه داشته باشید که مغز و ماهیچه‌های‌تان در حال یادگیری مطالب جدیدی هستند و این کار به تمرین زیاد نیاز دارد. بارها به فایل‌هایی که در وب‌سایت گذاشته شده گوش دهید و تمرین‌هایی را که برایتان مشکل بوده و در خانه نتوانسته بودید انجام دهید، دوباره مرور کنید. با این که بیشتر مطالبی که مطالعه می‌کنید با تصویر همراه هستند، به یاد داشته باشید که زبان اول‌تان را با شنیدن و گوش کردن یاد گرفتید، نه با خواندن و نوشتن. با وقت فراوانی که صرف گوش کردن به تمرین‌های شنیدن و انجام تمرین‌های دیکته می‌کنید، توانایی طبیعی خود در یادگیری زبان از راه شنیدن را دوباره تجربه کنید.

۳.

با صدای بلند مطالعه کنید. وقتی با مطالب این کتاب کار می‌کنید، به یک توانایی تکیه نکنید. گوش کنید و هم‌زمان تکرار کنید. تکرار کنید و شکل حرف یا واژه را تصور کنید. به جای این‌که در سکوت بنویسید، آنچه می‌نویسید را با صدای بلند تکرار کنید. مغز و دهان‌تان فقط با حرف زدن می‌توانند این زبان را فرا بگیرند؛ فکر کردن به زبان برای یادگیری آن کافی نیست! از هر فرصتی برای تمرین حرف زدن استفاده کنید، چه با همکلاسی‌تان، چه با سگ‌تان و چه با خودتان. بیشتر زبان‌آموزان موفق مرتب با خود حرف می‌زنند.

۴.

گروهی درس بخوانید. همیشه احتمال مطالعه‌ی فعال و ثمربخش در گروه بیشتر می‌شود. همه‌ی درس‌های این کتاب حاوی فعالیت‌هایی هستند که در گروه‌های دونفره بهتر اجرا می‌شوند. فعالیت‌های گروهی تأثیرگذار این کتاب، دیکته گفتن به یکدیگر، و ساختن جمله‌ها و گفت‌وگوهاست.

۵.

مطالعه و دوره کردن واژگان را در برنامه‌ی روزانه‌ی خود بگنجانید. یادگیری زبان یک فعالیت انباشتی است، بنابراین بسیار اهمیت دارد که واژه‌ها و اصطلاحات تازه را با مطالب قدیمی بیامیزید و هم‌بسته کنید. استفاده از مطالب تازه برای دوره کردن مطالب قدیمی به سازماندهی نیاز دارد، اما در نهایت، به روانی و توانایی چشمگیر در استفاده‌ی درست و به‌جا از زبان منجر خواهد شد. وقتی در حال یادگیری واژه‌ی جدیدی هستید، صداهایی که قبلاً یاد گرفته‌اید را مرور کنید. وقتی حروف جدیدی می‌آموزید، به عقب برگردید و تلاش کنید واژه‌هایی را که فقط شکل گفتاری آن‌ها را در گفت‌وگوها یاد گرفته بودید، به فارسی بنویسید. هر واژهٔ تازه را با یک واژهٔ قدیمی هم‌گروه کنید.

۶.

انتظار خستگی گاه و بیگاه را داشته باشید. خسته شدن علامت خوبی است: به این معناست که شما تمرکز کرده‌اید و ماهیچه‌های‌تان در حال تمرین و یادگیری تولید درست صداهای جدید است. به‌خاطر داشته باشید که آنچه در آغاز برای‌تان سخت است، به‌زودی آسان و آسان‌تر می‌شود.

تجربه‌ی یادگیری موفق و دل‌پذیری را برای‌تان آرزومندیم!

TIPS FOR USING THIS BOOK

1.

Prepare for active participation in class. To do this you need to spend time outside of class listening to and working with the audio and video exercises. Listen to and write the new sounds and letters as many times as you need to in order to feel comfortable recognizing and producing them. Prepare the lesson assigned beforehand, so that you will be ready to read and write. Class time should be spent practicing, not listening to lectures.

> **To access online resources: http://www.laits.utexas.edu/persian_teaching_resources/**

2.

Once is not enough. Whether you are pronouncing new sounds, writing new letters, or studying vocabulary, you should repeat the activity as many times as you can. Repeat until you can produce a sound or write a letter easily. Remember that you are training your brain and your muscles to do new things, and this takes practice. Listen to the materials on the website as many times as you can, and go back over items that you missed on the homework. Although most of your studies now are visually oriented, you learned your native language mainly through hearing and listening, and not through reading and writing. Rediscover your native ability to learn through listening by devoting as much time as you can to the listening and dictation exercises while working through this book.

3.

Study out loud. As you work through these materials, engage more than one faculty at the same time. Listen and repeat together. Repeat and picture the shape of the letter or word. Rather than write silently, repeat whatever you are writing out loud. The only way to train your brain and your mouth to speak this language is by doing; thinking about it is not enough! Practice speaking at every chance you get, whether with classmates, the dog, or yourself. Most successful language learners talk to themselves regularly.

4.

Study with others. You are much more likely to study actively when you study with a partner. Every lesson in this book contains activities that are best done in pairs. Good group activities include dictating to each other and making up sentences and dialogues.

5.

Make vocabulary study and review part of your day. Language is cumulative, and while you are learning new words and expressions, it is important to integrate the old in with them. Using the new to review the old will take some organization, but it will pay off in greater fluency and accuracy. When you learn new words, take the opportunity to work on previously learned sounds. When you learn new letters, go back to words you have learned only in spoken form to see if you can write any of it in Persian script. Pair up each new word with an old one.

6.

Expect to feel tired occasionally. Being tired is a good sign: it means that you are concentrating, and that you are training your muscles to produce new sounds correctly. Remember that you will soon be able to do easily things that tire you at first.

We wish you a successful and enjoyable learning experience!

سخنی با استادان

این کتاب درسی و جلدهای بعدی آن، بر اساس فلسفه آموزش و یادگیری زبان به شیوه‌ی ارتباطی و با به‌کارگیری اصول و شیوه‌های مدرن آموزش زبان طراحی و تدوین شده‌اند و هدف آن‌ها ارتقای مهارت‌های زبانی در زبان فارسی است. از شما استادان عزیز می‌خواهیم که این پیشگفتار، و نیز «سخنی با فارسی آموزان» را بخوانید و از دانشجویان خود هم بخواهید که این بخش‌ها را بخوانند؛ آنگاه در کلاس درباره آن‌چه که خوانده‌اند بحث و تبادل نظر کنید تا همه از قواعدی که ساختار و محتوای کتاب بر آن بنا شده، آگاه باشند.

در این جلد، معیار چینش در ارائه حروف الفبا، بسامد حروف و آسانی نوشتن بوده است. واژگان با توجه به میزان کاربردشان در زبان معرفی می‌شوند، نه بر اساس تقدّم الفبایی؛ اما از آن‌جا که زبان‌آموزان از ابتدا و به‌سرعت با حروف پربسامد فارسی آشنا می‌شوند، از همان روزهای اول قادر خواهند بود بیشتر واژه‌های هر درس را به فارسی بنویسند.

کتاب، از همان ابتدا، دانشجویان را با هر دو شیوه‌ی نوشتاری (رسمی) و گفتاری (غیر رسمی) زبان فارسی آشنا می‌کند، چرا که معتقد است سخن گفتن به یک زبان، زمانی به مرز بسندگی نزدیک می‌شود که زبان‌آموز بتواند از لحن‌های فرهنگی متنوع آن زبان، در موقعیت‌های مناسب استفاده کند. شیوه ارائه مطالب و تنوع آن‌ها به شما این امکان را می‌دهد که بر اساس برنامه‌های درسی و نیاز دانشجویان گونه‌ی رسمی یا غیر رسمی زبان فارسی را مبنای آموزش قرار دهید.

طراحی محتوای این کتاب به‌گونه‌ای ست که زبان‌آموزان بیشترین میزان آمادگی و یادگیری را بیرون از کلاس داشته باشند و در عوض، در کلاس به فعالیت‌های تعاملی، دیدن ویدیوها و تمرین گفتگوها، و تعامل واقعی با زبان فارسی (به جای شنیدن درباره آن) بپردازند.

همه‌ی مواد شنیداری-دیداری نسخه‌ی اول کتاب، در وب‌سایت آن، به آدرسی که پشت جلد کتاب آمده، در دسترس زبان‌آموزان است. ویدیوهای آموزش نوشتن الفبا و گفت‌وگوهای کوتاه نیز بخشی از این مجموعه‌اند.

در نگاه اول، شاید به‌نظر برسد آموزش الفبا که می‌تواند در چند جلسه به پایان برسد، در این کتاب به درازا کشیده است، اما باید توجه داشت که پربسامدترین حروف الفبا تا آخر درس پنجم آموزش داده شده و مهم‌تر آن که هدف جلد اول کتاب، آموزش همزمان همه مهارت‌هاست. زمانی که برای فراگیری الفبا به زبان‌آموزان می‌دهیم، نه تنها هیچ تأثیر منفی بر یادگیری زبان نخواهد داشت، مشکلات یادگیری مهارت نوشتن را به حداقل می‌رساند و به آن‌ها فرصت می‌دهد با اعتماد به نفس بیشتری شروع به نوشتن کنند. با استفاده از این کتاب و مواد صوتی- تصویری آن، آموزش الفبا در خانه و توسط خو زبان‌آموز صورت می‌گیرد. با استفاده از این کتاب و با مخاطب آشنا به زبان انگلیسی، می‌توانید از همان روزهای نخست کلاس با زبان‌آموزان به فارسی سخن بگویید.

بنا بر رویکرد آموزشی این کتاب، دانشجویان باید پیش از کلاس، نیروی زیادی صرف «آمادگی برای کلاس» کنند و در مقابل وقت کلاس باید صرف فعالیت‌های تعاملی در گروه‌های کوچک شود. با این شیوه می‌توان با به حداکثر رساندن مشارکت تک تک زبان‌آموزان در فعالیت‌های کلاس، تلاش‌های خارج از کلاس آن‌ها را به ثمر نشاند.

از آنجا که کتاب به شیوه‌ای طراحی شده که هر زبان‌آموز می‌تواند با سرعت مطلوب مطالب را بخواند و فرا گیرد، سرعت فراگیری افراد تأثیر چندانی بر روند کار کلاس نخواهد داشت. از سوی دیگر، این شیوه از آغاز به زبان‌آموزان می‌آموزد که یادگیری، وظیفه خود آن‌هاست، و به این ترتیب، آن‌ها را به یادگیری فعالانه عادت می‌دهد. نکته اساسی آخر این که آموزگار کلاس خود باید از

قواعدی که بنا نهاده به‌درستی پیروی کند، به این معنا که با آموزش مطالبی که قرار بوده پیش از کلاس خوانده شود، به دانشجوی ناآماده و کم‌تلاش پاداش ندهد و متقابلاً دانشجوی آماده و پرتلاش را نیازارد.

فعالیت‌های شنیدن، به عنوان آمادگی و تکلیف، پیش از کلاس انجام می‌شود. تمام فعالیت‌ها با برچسب‌های «درخانه» و «در کلاس» تفکیک شده‌اند. این نکته می‌تواند در تدوین طرح درس روزانه و هفتگی به شما کمک کند. پیشنهاد ما این است که برای هر جلسه‌ی کلاس به شکلی برنامه‌ریزی کنید که حداقل چند فعالیت هم‌کنشی (که دو طرف در آن به مبادله اطلاعات می‌پردازند) داشته باشید. با فراگیری واژه‌های بیشتر، این فعالیت‌ها به زمان بیشتری نیاز خواهند داشت. در فصل‌های انتهایی کتاب، انتظار می‌رود ۷۵ درصد وقت کلاس به این گونه فعالیت‌ها بگذرد. فعالیت‌های ویژه‌ی گروه‌های کوچک و گروه‌های دو نفره، نقشی بنیادی در ساخت و پرورش مهارت‌های زبانی دارند. درست و بی‌اشتباه سخن گفتن، با دریافت پاداش که همان لذت فراگیری است، تقویت می‌شود، اما این بدان معنا نیست که تک‌تک لغزش‌های زبانی زبان‌آموزان هنگام سخن گفتن در کلاس، باید اصلاح شود.

ما بر این باوریم که همه قادرند صداهای زبان فارسی را درست ادا کنند، پس لازم است از ابتدا زبان‌آموزان را به تولید صداهای درست تشویق کنیم و از آنها این توقع را داشته باشیم. چند درس نخست این جلد، برای شما و دانشجویان‌تان فرصتی فراهم می‌کند که از ابتدا بر جنبه آوایی زبان فارسی تمرکز کافی داشته باشید. رویکرد شما به عنوان آموزگار زبان فارسی باید این باشد که همه می‌توانند صداهای زبان فارسی را درست تولید کنند.

هر درس شامل یک بخش آموزش واژه است که فعالیت‌ها و تمرین‌های متعددی برای فعال کردن واژه‌های تازه در خود دارد. زبان‌آموزان باید پیش از آمدن به کلاس، تمرین‌های خانگی بخش واژگان را انجام دهند و به گفتگوها گوش کنند، تا برای فعالیت‌های مشابه کلاسی آماده شوند. در این مرحله، هدف این نیست که زبان‌آموز گفتگوها را بنویسد؛ بلکه این گفتگوها برای پرورش اعتماد به نفس وی در یادگیری مهارت شنیدن طراحی شده‌اند. بهتر است دانشجویان را تشویق کنیم که بیشتر بر حافظه آواشناختی خود تکیه کنند نه بر حافظه تصویری خود. همه‌ی انسان‌ها به طور طبیعی دارای مهارت‌های یادگیری شفاهی و شنیداری هستند و به‌یقین می‌توان گفت هیچ‌کس زبان اول خود را از راه خواندن یاد نگرفته است.

هر درس با یک یادداشت فرهنگی آغاز می‌شود، اما برنامه دقیقی برای آموزش این بخش معین نشده است تا بتوانید هر طور مایلید برای این بخش برنامه‌ریزی کنید و بر جنبه‌هایی که به نظرتان مهم می‌آید تمرکز کنید. هر طور می‌پسندید از ویدیوها، تصاویر تصویرها و یادداشت‌های فرهنگی به عنوان نقطه شروع برای طرح پرسش و آغاز بحث استفاده کنید. پیشنهاد ما این است که از زبان‌آموزان بخواهید هر گفتگو را چندین بار، به ترتیب زیر، گوش دهند:
۱) پیش از هر توضیحی، از آنها بخواهید نگاهی کلی به موضوع بیاندازند و سپس بپرسید چه دریافت کرده‌اند.
۲) از آنها بخواهید هر چند بار که لازم می‌دانند ویدیو را تماشا کنند، تا معلوم شود چه واژه‌ها یا عبارت‌هایی را می‌شنوند؛ سپس درباره آنها بحث کنند و در نهایت با کمک شما تمام گفتگو را دریابند.
۳) از آنها بخواهید برای آخرین بار نگاه کنند و بعد از اینکه متوجه شدند چه گفته می‌شود، بر این نکته که «چطور گفته می‌شود» تمرکز کنند. دانشجویان پس از طی این مراحل، باید آماده باشند که خود این عبارت‌ها را بیان کنند و بازمایند. به آنها فرصت دهید تا نمایشنامه کوتاه خودشان را با هر موقعیتی که دوست دارند، بسازند و آن را در کلاس اجرا کنند. مشارکت شما در کارآمدی این مواد آموزشی نقش بسزایی دارد.

PERSIAN OF IRAN TODAY

مواد آموزشی این کتاب را می‌توان به طور تقریبی در طول ۹۰ ساعت کلاسی به‌کار گرفت. این زمان با احتساب فعالیت‌هایی است که قرار است در کلاس انجام شود، و با این فرض که زمان کلاس به هیچ‌وجه به سخنرانی و توضیح نخواهد گذشت و از سوی دیگر دانشجویان هر شب یک تا دو ساعت به انجام تکلیف‌های خانگی خواهند پرداخت. بیشتر تمرین‌های کتاب قرار است در خانه انجام شوند پس تا آنجا که می‌توانید زمان کلاس را به فعالیت‌هایی بگذرانید که انجام‌شان بیرون از کلاس برای زبان‌آموز امکان‌پذیر نیست، مانند سخن گفتن و املا. در این روش آموزشی، دیکته از اهمیت زیادی برخوردار است، زیرا ما بر این باوریم که تسلط بر صداها و توانایی برقراری ارتباط میان صداها و حروف الفبا باید در مراحل اولیه یادگیری زبان پرورش یابد و تقویت شود. صداها و کلمه‌ها را مرتب تکرار کنید، و برای این‌که نگرانی و فشار اجرای فردی را از دوش زبان‌آموزان بردارید، از ایشان بخواهید به صورت گروهی صداها و واژه‌ها را تکرار کنند.

مجموع ساعت کلاسی در برنامه	تعداد هفته‌ای که برای اتمام ده درس لازم است	مجموع ساعات کار در خانه در طول هفته	مدت ساعت درسی در هفته
۹۰	۱۵	۱۲	۶
۹۰	۲۲-۲۳	۸	۴
۹۰	۳۰	۶	۳
تعداد ساعات لازم برای تکمیل			

به‌یقین، هیچ کتابی جای یک آموزگار خوب را نمی‌گیرد. ما امیدواریم که این مواد در پربارتر کردن کلاس به شما کمک کند و یادگیری زبان شیرین فارسی را برای دانشجویان‌تان تجربه‌ای دلپذیر سازد.

TO THE INSTRUCTOR

This textbook, and the continuing books in the Persian of Iran series, are constructed around a philosophy of teaching and learning Persian in a communicative manner designed to maximize students proficiency. We ask that you, the instructor, read this preface as well as the Preface to the Student, and that you have your students read the latter and discuss it with them in class, so that everyone understands the principles underlying the structure and contents of these materials.

In this volume, the alphabet is presented in a way designed to take advantage of both letter frequency and letter shape. Vocabulary is introduced according to function, not alphabet, but by presenting letters based on frequency, students will be able to write many of the words they learn using the Persian script from the beginning. In addition, we introduce our students to both formal and informal varieties, based on the principle that learning to speak in a culturally appropriate manner is a part of proficiency that should not be ignored. The extent to which you emphasize each variety will depend on your program and the needs of your students.

These materials are designed so that students can do most of the preparation and actual learning of new material outside of class, in order for class time to be spent doing interactive activities, watching and practicing conversations, and working with Persian (instead of hearing about it). In this first edition, students have available to them audiovisual materials on the website, including visual footage demonstrating how to write all the letters of the alphabet, and dialogues, whose texts are found in the Appendix.

We believe that it is crucial to expect a high degree of effort from students in preparing for class, and equally, that this effort must be rewarded by spending class time doing interactive and small-group activities that permit maximum participation by all students. Since the book is designed so that the students can do much of their learning outside of class, each person may work at his or her own pace, so that differences in learning speed need not affect the class as a whole. It is also important that students realize right away that the burden of learning is on them, because this helps them to become active learners. Finally, it is essential to follow through on the expectations you set. Do not reward students who have not prepared, and punish those who have, by "teaching" them what they should have done outside of class.

The listening exercises are all meant to be done outside class as part of homework and preparation. We have specified the drills that are meant to be done as homework and those that are meant to be done in class as interactive or small group exercises and projects. We suggest that, in preparing your lesson plans, you aim to have at least some interactive work each and every class period, and that the time set aside for this increases as students learn more vocabulary so that, by the end of the book, you are spending 75% of class time with students working together speaking directly with each other. Small group work and pair work is essential for students to build skills. Accuracy will improve if students see it rewarded, and it will not suffer if we do not correct every single utterance.

We believe that everyone can produce Persian sounds accurately and that it is necessary to encourage and even to expect accuracy from the outset. These early units are an opportunity for you and the students to focus all of your attention on the phonetic aspects of Persian, and it is also better to form good habits from the start. Your attitude as a teacher of Persian should be that everyone can learn to produce these sounds accurately.

Each unit includes a vocabulary section complete with several exercises and activities that activate new words. Students should prepare the vocabulary and listen to dialogues on the website before class and be prepared to perform similar tasks in class. At this stage, it is not our goal for the students to write out the dialogues. Instead, it is good training for the students to develop confidence in their aural and oral skills at this stage, and they need to be encouraged to rely on their "phonographic" rather than their "photographic" memory. Everyone has natural aural and oral language learning skills; no one learned her or his native language through reading.

While we have included short cultural notes in the book, we have not provided detailed lesson plans in order to give you the flexibility to proceed as you wish and focus on the aspects you deem important. Use the videos, pictures, and cultural notes as starting points to encourage questions and discussion, and expand as you wish. We suggest that you have students listen to each dialogue several times as follows: (1) Before explaining anything, have them watch for general content, then ask what they understood. (2) Have them watch again, as many times as necessary, to listen for individual words or expressions, followed by discussion and explanation of what they heard. (3) Have them watch a final time, after they have understood what is said, to focus on how it is said. After that, the students should be ready to try out the expressions themselves, so let them make up their own situations and act them out. Your own contribution will be vital to the success of these materials.

The material in this textbook can be covered well in approximately ninety contact hours, depending on the amount of time devoted to the various activities, assuming class time is not spent on lectures and students will devote one to two hours a night to homework. Most of the exercises in the textbook are meant to be done as homework. Spend as much class time as possible on activities that students cannot complete at home alone; such activities might include speaking and dictation. This approach stresses dictation because we believe that the mastery of sounds and the ability to relate sounds and writing must be developed early. Repeat sounds and words many times over, and have students repeat as a group to take the pressure off individual performance.

Contact Hours per Week	Homework Hours per Week	Number of Weeks to Complete Units 1-10	Total Contact Hours
6	12	15	90
4	8	22-23	90
3	6	30	90
Hours to Completion			

Of course, no textbook can take the place of a good teacher. It is our hope that these materials will help you to enrich your classroom and make learning Persian an enjoyable experience for your students.

INTRODUCTION

The Persian Alphabet

The Persian alphabet contains thirty-two letters consisting of consonants and vowels, and eight symbols that function as vowels and pronunciation markers, or as markers of certain grammatical functions. Units One through Ten will introduce these letters and symbols individually.

First, take a look at the alphabet in the chart below, which shows the thirty-two letters. Starting in the upper right-hand corner, the chart reads across from right to left, which is the direction Persian is written and read. To see and hear the pronunciation of these letters, listen to Introduction-1 on the website.

ت	پ	ب	ا
ح	چ	ج	ث
ر	ذ	د	خ
ش	س	ژ	ز
ظ	ط	ض	ص
ق	ف	غ	ع
م	ل	گ	ک
ی	ه	و	ن

The next chart shows the eight extra-alphabetical symbols. They include vowels, pronunciation symbols, and grammatical endings. These symbols will be introduced in Units One through Ten along with the alphabet.

ؔ	ؕ	ؙ
ؗ	ء	ؖ
	آ	ؘ

Special Characteristics of the Persian Script

The Persian writing system has several major characteristics that distinguish it from its European counterparts:

1. Persian is written from right to left. One consequence of this ordering system is that Persian books, newspapers, and magazines open and are read in the opposite direction from European and American printed materials.

2. Letters are connected in both print and handwriting. Unlike languages written in the Latin alphabet, which are generally connected only in certain types of handwriting, Persian letters are written connected in both print and handwriting. The following are individual letters which are written one after the other in correct order, but which do not form a word written this way:

ن ا ن

When they are connected, however, they do spell a word "نان" /nân/ which means bread.

Notice that not all the letters in connect to the following letter. This is a characteristic of certain letters that you will master as you learn to write. See if you can identify the non-connecting letters in the following words:

سرد	مادر	زن	دوست	وقت

As you learn the alphabet, note which letters connect and which do not, and when you write words, do not lift the pen or pencil from the page until you get to a natural break with a non-connecting letter.

3. Letters have slightly different shapes depending on where they occur in a word. The chart on the next page gives the forms of the letters when written independently; these forms vary when the letters are written in initial/medial and final position. "Initial position" means not connected to a previous letter, "medial position" is usually written the same as the initial position, except that it is connected to the previous letter, and "final position" means connected to the preceding letter only. Most letters have a particularly distinct shape when they occur in final position, similar to the way English can have capital letters at the beginning of words. The chart below gives you an idea of the extent of this variation. You will see that each letter retains a basic shape throughout; this is the core of the letter. If the letter has dots, their number and position also remain the same. Note that the last three letters, which all connect, appear to have a "tail" in their independent and final forms which drops off when they are connected and is replaced by a connecting segment that rests on the line. Try to find the core shape of each letter, its dots, if any, the connecting segments, and the final tail in the following chart.

Final Position	Initial/Medial Position	Independent Shape
ا	ا ، ا	ا
ت	ت ، ت	ت
ج	ج ، ج	ج
ع	ع ، ع	ع

As you learn each letter of the alphabet, you will learn to read and write all its various shapes. You will be surprised how quickly you master them with a little practice!

4. Persian script consists of two separate "layers" of writing. The basic skeleton of a word is made up of the consonants and the three vowels that have alphabetic forms, which were historically called long vowels following the Arabic tradition. The other three vowels, historically called short vowels, and other pronunciation and grammatical markers are separated from the consonant skeleton of the word. This second layer, called vocalization, is normally omitted in writing, and the reader recognizes words without it. Compare the following two versions of the same text, a line of poetry, the second of which represents the normal way of writing, without vocalization, and the first of which has all the pronunciation markers added:

$$\text{به جَهان خُرَّم اَز آنَم که جَهان خُرَّم اَز اوست}$$

Most books, magazines, and newspapers are unvocalized, as the following text demonstrates.

$$\text{به جهان خرّم از آنم که جهان خرّم از اوست}$$

In unvocalized texts, there may be several possible pronunciations for one written word; however, because of context this rarely results in ambiguous word meaning. On the other hand, the meaning of a phrase may not be immediately apparent to the reader because of unwritten grammatical markers, such as the ezafe marker, which will be covered in Unit Four. For this reason, reading a text aloud without prior preparation may be difficult.

In this textbook series, vocalization marks will be used when new vocabulary is introduced, but thereafter you will be expected to have memorized the pronunciation of the word, and these marks will be omitted. Since Persian speakers normally read and write without vocalization, it is best to become accustomed to reading and writing that way from the beginning.

Notes On The Pronunciation Of Persian

In addition to the characteristics of the Persian script, you should also be aware of certain features of the sounds of Persian.

1. Persian does not have a one-to-one correspondence between sound and letter. Due to historical reasons, many Arabic words have been borrowed into Persian, including their original Arabic spelling. The pronunciation of these words has been modified to fit the Persian sound system, which contains fewer consonants than Arabic, meaning that there are multiple ways of writing certain sounds in Persian. For example, both Persian and Arabic have a letter ز /z/ in their writing and sound systems, but the letters ذ ض ظ , which represent different sounds in Arabic, are all pronounced as ز /z/ in Persian.

2. The Persian writing system is regularly phonetic, which means that words are generally written as they are pronounced. American English speakers sometimes confuse pronunciation and spelling without realizing it. For example, think about the word television. This word has been adopted into Persian and is pronounced something like televizyun. It is also spelled with the Persian letter that corresponds to the sound z, because that is the way it is pronounced. English spelling, on the other hand, requires an s, even though there is no s sound in the word. Pay attention to the sounds of the Persian letters, and avoid associating English letters with them. Learn to recognize and pronounce the sounds correctly now, and not only will you avoid spelling problems, but you will also learn and retain vocabulary more easily.

3. Most Persian consonantal sounds are similar to sounds you already know. Many of the sounds of Persian are similar to sounds present in English, but do not assume that they are exactly the same. Pay attention to what parts of the mouth you must use to produce these sounds properly from the beginning, when you are able to focus the most attention on them. Just as you must train your arm to hit a tennis ball, you must train your mouth to make the Persian sounds properly. Do not allow yourself to speak lazily, as that will hinder your ability to speak with good pronunciation. Keep your mind on the sounds you are making at all times. With practice, you will be able to do this with less and less effort.

Persian sounds are produced with a pulmonic egressive airstream mechanism. Modern Tehran Persian has twenty-three consonantal and seven vocalic phonemes (six vowels and one diphthong). In the following tables of vocalic and consonantal phonemes, IPA symbols, when different from our notation, are given in parentheses.

4. Persian vowel sounds: You may have been taught in school that English has five vowels: a, e, i, o, u. This is true of the English writing system, but in speech, English has many possible vowel sounds, which are ambiguously represented in our writing system by only these five symbols. Compare, for example, the vowel quality in each of the following words: book, bug, blue, black, bother, beep, bed, bid. In contrast, Persian has only six vowel sounds.

Table 3.1

PERSIAN VOCALIC PHONEMES		
	front	back
high	i	u
mid	e (ɛ)	o
low	æ	a
diphthong		ow (ou)

Shahrzad Mahootian, P: 286
Persian. Routledge Descriptive Grammars
Routledge, London, Great Britain, 1997.

5. Word stress: The stress in Persian words generally falls on the last syllable of a word, with few exceptions. You will learn the other rules for stress as they become necessary.

6. Word-final shortening: You will probably notice in class that when a word ends in two consonants, the second consonant will not be pronounced heard clearly. For example, the word [pokht] is pronounced [pokhd]. You'll learn more about this later in the book.

A Note on Transcription

While you are learning the alphabet, you will learn to say some words before you learn to write them in Persian. Using transcription should be a temporary, transitional stage, and you should move to writing only in Persian as soon as possible. Do not let transcription become a crutch!

Units One through Ten

In Units One through Ten, you will learn the basics of reading, writing, and speaking Persian. Listen to the audio files as you read, make a habit of pronouncing out loud everything you write while you are writing it, and practice on your own in addition to doing the exercises in the book. The more time you put in now, the easier it will be to learn vocabulary, pronounce and spell words correctly, and speak and read fluently.

Introductory Exercise

Listen to the audio file. You hear the pronunciation of the words with their meaning in English. Write the English words you hear. Which words sound familiar to you? Some of the words you hear are the words you will learn in the first 10 units.

Symbol used in the book for transcribing Persian words	English Words with Similar Sounds	Persian Word with the Sound at the End	Persian Word with the Sound in the Middle	Persian Word with the Sound at the Beginning
â	arm, father, hot	۳. شما	۲. مادر	۱. آره
a	cat, black	۶. برادر	۵. سرد	۴. از
e	met, bed	۹. خانه	۸. پدر	۷. امتحان
i	hit, sitting, see, heat	۱۲. داری	۱۱. پیر	۱۰. ایران
o	four, go, home	۱۵. دو	۱۴. کجا	۱۳. اتاق
u	blue, food, put, could	۱۸. دارو	۱۷. شور	۱۶. او
ow	oh!, row		۲۰. رو	۱۹. نوروز
b	bad, lab	۲۳. آب	۲۲. صبح	۲۱. بله
d	did, lady	۲۶. استاد	۲۵. مداد	۲۴. دانشجو
f	find, if	۲۹. کیف	۲۸. دفتر	۲۷. فردا
g	give, flag	۳۲. بزرگ	۳۱. زندگی	۳۰. گربه
gh/q	This sound is similar to the sound you made when you were a kid and you would gulp water	۳۵. شلوغ	۳۴. شغل	۳۳. قالی، غار
h	how, hello	۳۸. ده	۳۷. ناهار	۳۶. هفت

Symbol Used in the Book for Transcribing Persian Words	English Words with Similar Sounds	Persian Word with the Sound at the End	Persian Word with the Sound in the Middle	Persian Word with the Sound at the Beginning
y	yes, yellow	۴۱. چای	۴۰. عید	۳۹. یک
k	cat, back	۴۴. یک	۴۳. آمریکا	۴۲. کشور
l	leg, little	۴۷. صندل	۴۶. کلاس	۴۵. لب
m	man, lemon	۵۰. سلام	۴۹. امّا	۴۸. من
n	no, ten	۵۳. زن	۵۲. صندلی	۵۱. نه
p	pet, map	۵۶. سوپ	۵۵. سوپر مارکت	۵۴. پیر
r	red, try	۵۹. دور	۵۸. مرد	۵۷. روز
s	sun, miss	۶۲. مهندس	۶۱. دوست	۶۰. سلام
sh	she, crash	۶۵. ورزش	۶۴. تشنه	۶۳. شام
t	tea, getting	۶۸. هشت	۶۷. دختر	۶۶. تو
ch	check, church	۷۱. هیچ	۷۰. کوچک	۶۹. چای
v	voice, five	۷۴. گاو	۷۳. دوازده	۷۲. ورزش
kh	Listen to the audio file to hear this sound	۷۷. میخ	۷۶. می‌خورم	۷۵. خوب
zh	/zh/, as in mirage	۸۰. گاراژ	۷۹. مژه	۷۸. ژاپن
z	zoo, lazy	۸۳. میز	۸۲. روزنامه	۸۱. زن
'	Glottal stop. Say "uh-oh!" In between "uh" and "oh" there is a glottal stop.			۸۴. ساعت

درس اوّل
UNIT 1

سلام، حال شما چه طوره؟ — Hi, how are you?
اسم شما چیه؟ — What is your name?

Cultural Note — یادداشت فرهنگی

سلام و احوالپرسی ۱   Greetings 1

"سلام، حال شما چه‌طوره؟" [Salâm, hâl-e shomâ chetore?] is the most common way to greet someone in everyday conversation. The phrase literary means "Hello, how are you?" and it is a polite and formal way to start an interaction with someone. Persian greetings are usually long and detailed. They may consist of several exchanges and often include questions about family as well. However, sometimes this phrase is used as a quick greeting as familiar faces pass one another in a hallway of an office or on the street. In such cases, people may use the shortened version of the phrase "سلام، حال شما؟" [Salâm, hâl-e shomâ ?] The answer to such a quick greeting is usually equally as short, such as "سلام، ممنونم" [Salâm, mamnunam] or "سلام، خوب! شما چطورین؟" [Salâm, khub! shomâ chetorin?]. When two women greet each other saying "سلام، حال شما چطوره؟" [Salâm, hâl-e shomâ chetore?], they usually shake hands. If they already know each other well, they also often kiss twice, once on each cheek. Men usually greet another in the same fashion, shaking hands and kissing on the cheeks. However, men and women do not shake hands or kiss one another, unless they are mahram to each other (i.e. brother and sister, father and daughter, husband and wife, or uncle and niece), or if they know each other well enough and know that it is appropriate to do so.

Short Conversations — گفتگوهای کوتاه

In class, listen to the audio files and transcribe the conversations. At home repeat what you hear several times and try to follow the rhythm. During the next class time, you will work with a classmate to create a scenario that uses these expressions.

متن فارسی این گفتگوها در انتهای کتاب نوشته شده است.

....

....

-..................................

....

. esme shomâ chiye?

. esme man samâne ast.

آ...ا...	ب...ب...	پ...پ...	ت...ت...	ن...ن...	و...	ی...ی...	ـَ ـِ ـُ

This unit will introduce you to seven letters of the Persian alphabet as well as the vowel symbols.

Part 1: alef /â/ آ ‎ ا

آسمان	سراب	دریا

❋ **Note:** These words show how alef appears in different positions in a word. You do not need to know how to read these words.

1. Listen to the audio file for آ alef.

The name of the first letter of the Persian alphabet is *alef*. *Alef* has two main functions, the first of which will be introduced here, and the second of which will be introduced later in this unit. For now, *alef* represents the vowel sound /â/. This sound is a deep, open sound, somewhat similar to the a in talk or father but with a bit of the sound /o/ in it. Note that *alef* does not connect to the letter that follows it.

2. Watch the video and follow the instructions.

آ ....

ا ....

3. Mark X for each word you hear /â/.

☐ ۳.   ☐ ۲.   ☐ ۱.

☐ ۵.   ☐ ۴.

4. Circle آ or ا in the text. Report to your instructor how many " ا / آ " you identified in the text?

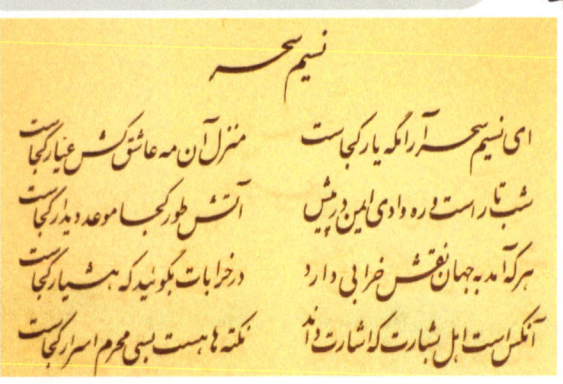

5. Numbers in Persian: Like English they are written and read from left to right.

Number in English	Persian equivalent	Pronunciation in Persian
0	۰	/sefr/
1	۱	/yek/
2	۲	/do/
3	۳	/se/
4	۴	/châhâr/ (/châr/)
5	۵	/panj/

6. Watch the video and write the numbers in Persian three times. Read them aloud as you write.

۱-۲-۳-۴-۵ ....

....

7. Listen to the audio file and write the number you hear.

۱. ....   ۲. ....   ۳. ....   ۴. ....   ۵. ....

۶. ....   ۷. ....   ۸. ....   ۹. ....   ۱۰. ....

8. Listen to the audio file and check the number that you hear.

۱. ☐ ۱ ☐ ۳ ☐ ۵   ۲. ☐ ۴ ☐ ۲ ☐ ۳   ۳. ☐ ۵ ☐ ۵ ☐ ۱

۴. ☐ ۲ ☐ ۴ ☐ ۳   ۵. ☐ ۳ ☐ ۱ ☐ ۲

Part 2: be /b/ ____ب____

| باز | شب | مبارک |

1. Listen to the audio file for ب be.

The second letter of the Persian alphabet, be, is pronounced like the English "b." Unlike alef, this is a connecting letter, which means that it connects to any letter following it in the same word.

2. Watch the video and follow the instructions.

ب ....

ب ....

3. Watch the video and write the following words.

با ....

آب ....

باب ....

4. Listen and check when you hear the /b/ sound in the word.

۱. ☐   ۲. ☐   ۳. ☐   ۴. ☐   ۵. ☐

5. Circle the letter ب in the following text. Report to your instructor how many "ب" you identified in the text.

زبان و خط رسمی و مشترک مردم ایران فارسی است. اسناد و مکاتبات و متون رسمی و کتب درسی باید با این زبان و خط باشد ولی استفاده از زبان‌های محلی و قومی در مطبوعات و رسانه‌های گروهی و تدریس ادبیات آنها در مدارس، در کنار زبان فارسی آزاد است.

اصل پانزدهم قانون اساسی جمهوری اسلامی ایران

فصل دوم: زبان، خط، تاریخ و پرچم رسمی کشور

Text from Iran's Constitution

6. Listen and write the numbers you hear.

۱.   ۲.   ۳.   ۴.   ۵.

Part 3: nun /n/ ___ن___ | نَمَک | سَنگ | نان |

1. Listen to the audio file for ن *nun*.

The letter *nun* is pronounced like the English "n." *Nun* is a connecting letter whose shape resembles that of ب in initial and medial positions, except for the placement of the dot, which comes above the tooth. It differs from ب in that the independent and final forms of ن take a characteristic "tail" shape that dips well below the line.

2. Watch the video and follow the instructions.

ن .... نـ ....

3-1. Watch the video and write the following words.

نان .... بَنا ....

آبان .... بان ....

3-2. Watch the video and write the following words.

ناب .... آن ....

4. Listen and check when you hear /n/ sound in the word.

۱. ☐   ۲. ☐   ۳. ☐   ۴. ☐   ۵. ☐

5. Watch the video and write the numbers in Persian four times. Read them aloud as you write. Use the chart on the left as a pronunciation guide.

۶-۷-۸-۹-۱۰

....
....
....
....

Number in English	Persian equivalent	Pronunciation in Persian
6	۶	/shesh/ (/shish/)
7	۷	/haft/
8	۸	/hasht/
9	۹	/noh/
10	۱۰	/dah/

6. Listen to the audio and write the number you hear.

۱. ....   ۲. ....   ۳. ....   ۴. ....   ۵. ....

7. Circle the letter ن in the following text. Report to your instructor how many "ن" you identified in the text.

عکس‌هایی که می‌گیری

و موضوعاتی که برمی‌گزینی،

شخص درون تو را آشکار می‌کند.

میزان نزدیکی تو به موضوعات،

نشان از اشتیاق تو به آنهاست .

8. Listen and repeat.

۱-۲-۳-۴-۵-۶-۷-۸-۹-۱۰

9. Listen to the audio file and write the word you hear.

۵.　　　　　۴.　　　　　۳.　　　　　۲.　　　　　۱.

Part 4: zebar, zir, pish /a, e, o/

1. Watch the video and listen to the audio file for ِ a e o vowel markings

As you learned in the introduction, Persian has six vowel sounds, but only three of them have alphabetic equivalents. Three of the vowel sounds in Persian are indicated in Persian by markings written above or below the shape of the word. By convention, these vowels are written above or below the consonant they follow. Writing vowels is the third and final step in writing a word, after both the skeleton and the dots have been completed. Although at the beginning of words, these markers sit on or under an *alef*, these vowels are usually not written at all; they are generally used only in teaching language and for unfamiliar words.

The names of these vowel symbols are *zebar*َ , *zir*ِ , and *pish*ُ .

1. *Zebar*, which is written as a diagonal dash above the letter, sounds like the a sound in apple.
2. *Zir* is written as a diagonal dash below the letter. It is pronounced like the "e" in "bet."
3. Lastly, *pish* is written similar to a small, diagonal number 9 above the letter. It sounds like a pure letter "o," not like the English "o," which often has a hidden "u" sound after it. Try pronouncing the word boat slowly. The lips round at the end of the "o" sound, becoming more like a "u." The Persian pish is only the pure "o" sound, without the "u."

	اَبر	سَلام	شَب
	اِستخر	دِرخت	کِتاب
	اُتاق	بُزُرگ	کُرد

2-1. Watch the video and follow the instructions.

بَ ... بِ ... بُ ....

اَ ... اِ ... اُ ....

2-2. Watch the video and follow the instructions.

نان .... بُن ....

بَنا .... اُبا ....

اِنا .... اَبنا ....

3. Listen and check when you hear the /a/ sound in the word (as opposed to /â/).

□ ۱.   □ ۲.   □ ۳.   □ ۴.   □ ۵.

4. Mark X for each word in which you hear /â/ (as opposed to /a/).

□ ۱.   □ ۲.   □ ۳.   □ ۴.   □ ۵.

5. Listen and write the words you hear.

۱.   ۲.   ۳.   ۴.   ۵.

۶.   ۷.   ۸.   ۹.   ۱۰.

9 PERSIAN OF IRAN TODAY

6. Listen to the audio file and check the numbers that you hear.

۱.	☐ ۶	☐ ۷	☐ ۱
۲.	☐ ۴	☐ ۳	☐ ۹
۳.	☐ ۱	☐ ۵	☐ ۲
۴.	☐ ۱۰	☐ ۲	☐ ۵
۵.	☐ ۸	☐ ۱۰	☐ ۳
۶.	☐ ۹	☐ ۶	☐ ۴
۷.	☐ ۵	☐ ۱	☐ ۷
۸.	☐ ۳	☐ ۵	☐ ۱۰
۹.	☐ ۱	☐ ۹	☐ ۶
۱۰.	☐ ۲	☐ ۴	☐ ۸

7. Read the following words with your partner.

۱. أَبا

۲. آبان

۳. بابان

۴. اِبن

۵. أَبْنا

8. Circle the following vowel markings in the following text from the Quran.

9. Homework: Memorize giving your phone number digit by digit. While someone would not actually give his phone number this way in Persian, your goal for now is to review numbers 1-10.

10. In class: Ask your classmates for their phone numbers. Write their names and numbers in the list. Use this question to ask for their numbers: shomâre-ye telefonetun chand-e?

شماره‌ی تلفنتون چنده؟

نام	شماره‌ی تلفن

شماره‌ی تلفنم:

Shomâreye telefonam:

Part 5: pe, te /p/, /t/

ـپـ ـپ پ
| پنیر | بِپر | توپ |

ـتـ ـت ت
| توپ | کتاب | بست |

1. Listen to the audio file for پ pe ت te.

پ pe: The name of the next letter is pe, which is pronounced like the English /p/. It is written exactly like ب but with three dots below it.

ت te: The next letter, te, is pronounced like a clear, frontal English "t" like in Tom.

2. Writing پ and ت : Watch the video and follow the instructions.

پ ـپ ....

ت ـتـ ....

3. Watch the videos and write the following words.

پاپ .... نَبات .... تابان ....

اِتان .... آبان .... آن ....

آتِن .... بَنا .... پا ....

PERSIAN OF IRAN TODAY

4. Because *pe* and *te* are familiar sounds, let's continue working on distinguishing between /a/ and /â/. Listen and check when you hear the /â/ sound in the word (as opposed to /a/).

☐ ۱.   ☐ ۲.   ☐ ۳.   ☐ ۴.   ☐ ۵.

5. Circle the letters پ and ت in the following texts. Report to your instructor how many پ and ت you identified in the text.

درین سرای بی‌کسی کسی به در نمی‌زند
به دشتِ پُرملالِ ما پرنده پَر نمی‌زند

یکی ز شب گرفتگان چراغ بر نمی‌کند
کسی به کوچه سارِ شب درِ سحر نمی‌زند

نشسته‌ام در انتظارِ این غبارِ بی‌سوار
دریغ کز شبی چنین سپیده سر نمی‌زند

6. Listen and write the words you hear.

۱.   ۲.   ۳.   ۴.   ۵.

۶.   ۷.   ۸.   ۹.   ۱۰.

7. Connect the letters to form words as shown in the example. Sound the words out as you write them.

نَ + ب + ا + ت   →   نَبات......

بَ + ن + ا + ن   →   ....

بُ + ن   →   ....

ت + ا + ب + ا + ن   →   ....

آ + تِ + ن   →   ....

8. In class, read the following words with your partner.

۱. تاب	۲. آبان	۳. تابان	۴. بَنا	۵. پاپ
۶. آتِن	۷. نَبات	۸. نان	۹. آنان	۱۰. پا
۱۱. بُن	۱۲. تُن			

Part 6: ye /y/, /i/ ‍ـای ‍ـیـ یـ ایـ

ایران	بیدار	آبی	سورمه‌ای

1. Listen to the audio file for ی ye.

The letter ye is the first of four letters that function as both a consonant and a vowel. It functions as a consonant at the beginning of a word, or when preceded or followed by a vowel. In these cases, it is pronounced like /y/ in "yes." When it functions as a vowel, it sounds like the /i/ in feet. Notice that the initial and medial shapes are similar to those shapes of the letter ب only with two dots below. In the independent and final forms, it has a long tail that goes well below the line before coming back up to the level of the line. In independent and final positions, the two dots under the letter are not written. A ی at the beginning of a word makes the /y/ sound. In order to get an /i/ sound at the beginning of a word we use the combination ایـ (alef + ye).

2. Writing ی : Watch the video and follow the instructions.

یـ......ـیـ......ی

Written	Pronounced	Ex.	Pronounced	Note
ایـ	i	اینان	inân	
آی	ây	آیدا	âydâ	
اَی	ay	ایّام	ayyâm	There are only a few words that start with "اَی"
اِی	ey	ای	ey	There are only a few words that start with "اِی"
اُی	oy	ای	oy	There are a few words that start with "اُی"

13　PERSIAN OF IRAN TODAY

3-1. Watch the video and write the following words.

اینان .... بیب .... بی ....

بیَان .... یاب .... تی ....

پِی .... پایان ....

3-2. Watch the video and write the following words.

بیا .... پای ....

آی .... اِی ....

4. Listen and check when you hear the /i/ sound in the word (as opposed to /e/).

☐ ۱.   ☐ ۲.   ☐ ۳.   ☐ ۴.   ☐ ۵.

5. Circle the letter ی in the following text. Report to your instructor how many ی you identified in the text.

6. Listen and write the words you hear.

۱.   ۲.   ۳.   ۴.   ۵.

۶.   ۷.   ۸.   ۹.   ۱۰.

7. Listen and repeat the words you hear. Pay close attention to the sounds.
In class, read the following words with your partner.

۵. پات	۴. پُت	۳. پَت	۲. پِت	۱. پیت
۱۰. نُت	۹. نَت	۸. نات	۷. نِت	۶. نیت
۱۵. ایب	۱۴. یِب	۱۳. یَب	۱۲. یُب	۱۱. یاب

8. Read the following words with your partner.

۴. نَت / نُت	۳. پَت / پُت / پات	۲. نیت / نِت / نات	۱. پیت / پِت
	۶. یِب / یَب / یاب		۵. یاب / یُب

Part 7: *vâv* /u/, /o/

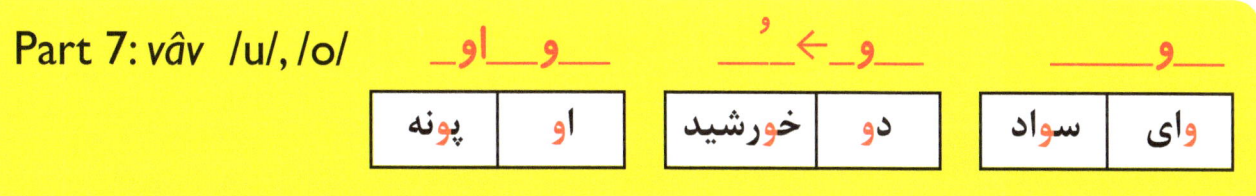

1. Listen to the audio file for و *vâv*.

This letter also functions as both a consonant and a vowel. When it is used as a consonant, it is pronounced /v/. When و is used as a vowel, it is pronounced /u/ or /o/. As a vowel, *vâv* is most often pronounced as an /u/. When it is pronounced as an /o/ we have the option of marking it with a *pish* in vocalized texts. Like *alef*, this letter does not connect to any following letter, so its shape does not change much.

Like ی the letter و is interpreted as a consonant sound when it is at the beginning of a word. In order to get an /u/ sound at the beginning of a word, we must use the combination او (*alef* + *vâv*).

2. Writing و : Watch the video and follow the instructions.

و ....

3. Watch the video and write the following words.

بو .... تَوان ....

او .... وَبا ....

4. Listen and check when you hear the /o/ sound in the word (as opposed to /u/).

۱. ☐   ۲. ☐   ۳. ☐   ۴. ☐   ۵. ☐   ۶. ☐

5. Circle the letter و in the following text. Report to your instructor how many و you identified in the text.

6. Listen and write the words you hear.

۱. ....

۲. ....

۳. ....

۴. ....

۵. ....

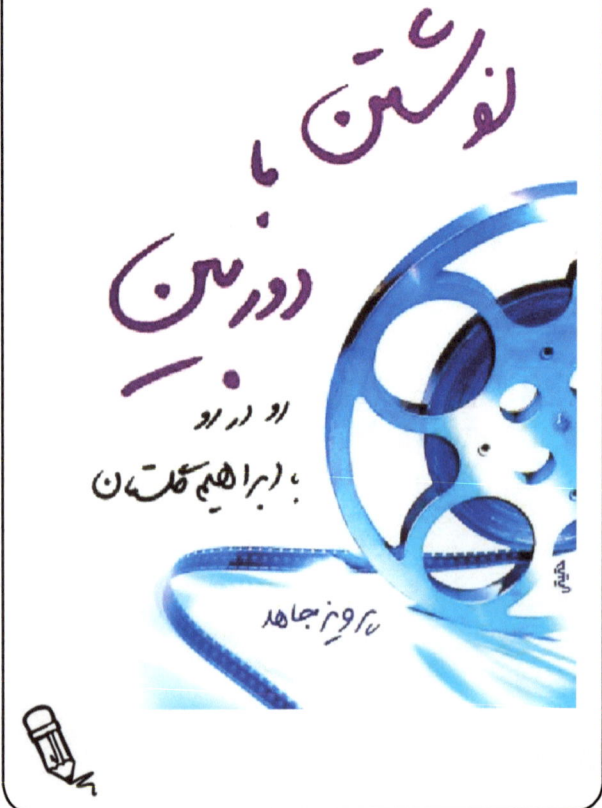

7. In class, read the following words with your partner.

۵. تو	۴. ناوی	۳. تاوان	۲. آبان	۱. آوا
۱۰. اونا	۹. توپ	۸. اون	۷. اوت	۶. توبا

8. Connect the letters to form words and read them after you have connected them.

۱. ا + ن + ی + ن ....

۲. اِ + ی ....

۳. بَ + ی + ا + ن ....

۴. پ + ا + ی + ا + ن ....

۵. آ + ب + ی ....

۶. ی + و + ن + ا + ن ....

9. Listen to the following words. Write the missing letters in the blank and rewrite the word.

۶. بـ ـا	۱. آ ـ ا ـ ....
۷. آبـ ـ	۲. پ ـ ـ پ ....
۸. وا ـ ت	۳. تـ ـ ا ـ ا ـ ....
۹. آ ـ ی	۴. و ـ ی ....
۱۰. تـ ـ ان	۵. نَـ ـ ات ....

10. In class, read the following words with your partner.

۵. آوِز	۴. آواز	۳. اِوَز	۲. اَوَز	۱. آواز
۱۰. اُوِز	۹. اُوَز	۸. آوَز	۷. اَواز	۶. اِواز

PERSIAN OF IRAN TODAY

واژگان Vocabulary

1. Listen to and learn these words. The spoken variations have been included in parentheses.

In order to write several sentences below you need to know how to write the word "is" (/ast/) in Persian. س is called *sin* and it corresponds to the English /s/ as in the word "seen." You can check to see how it is written in Unit 2 before you read the following sentences. When you have finished Unit 2, come back and review the following words.

this	این رایان است. (این رایانه.)	۱. این
that	آن نان، نان ایرانی است. (اون نون، نون ایرانیه.)	۲. آن (اون)
Iran	این ایران است (این ایرانه.)	۳. ایران
is	این سارا است. (این ساراست.)	۴. است (ه/ست)
bread	این نانِ ایرانی است.	۵. نان (نون)

2. Listen to the audio file again. Based on what you hear, write the vowels on the example sentences. Now listen to the next audio file. Write the sentences you hear and translate them to English.

درک شنیدار Listening Comprehension

1. Watch Videos 1-3 and transcribe the conversation you hear.

....

....

....

....

2. Watch Videos 4 and 5 and answer the following questions in Persian.

1– What is the girl's name?

2– Do you hear any numbers? What are they?

PERSIAN OF IRAN TODAY

Grammar Note   یادداشت دستوری

1. A Note on Names

Many Iranian family names end with /i/:

Karimi

Milani

Shushtari

Think of 5 Iranian last names you know which end with /i/ and write them here (in English).

۴. ....   ۱. ....

۵. ....   ۲. ....

۳. ....

2. Derivation

Since Persian is an Indo-European language, its structure is similar to that of English and other related languages. Like English, Persian words consist of word stems, prefixes, and suffixes, all of which change the meaning of the word. Look at the following sets of words in English and see if you can identify the different parts of the words.

Likeness, likely, unlikely, likelihood
Spain, Spanish
Activity, hyperactive

What this means for you as a learner of Persian is that you will be able to leverage the structure of the language to your benefit. As you learn more of the word-building pieces (stems, prefixes, and suffixes), you will be able to learn new words more quickly and even create words from roots, prefixes and suffixes you know. The first suffix we will look at is /i/. Look at the following words in transcription and try to guess how the /i/ at the end of the words changes the meaning of the stem word in this context.

/tehrân/ (Tehran), /tehrâni/
/arab/ (Arab), /arabi/
/bârân/ (rain), /bârâni/

3. Word Stress

Listen to the following words.

ایرانی
سلام
دانشجو

In Persian the stress generally falls on the final syllable of the word. The exceptions include verbs, conjunctions, indefinite nouns, and the interrogative particle "âyâ," among others. We will examine these exceptions in future units.

4. Syllable Structure

Written form in English	Pronunciation
Firouz	Fi/ruz
Firouzeh	Fi/ru/ze
Omid/Omeed	O/mid

Syllables in Persian

Syllables may be structured as C V (C) (C)*

* C = Consonant, V = Vowel

One syllable in each word (or breath group) is stressed, and knowing the rules is conducive to proper pronunciation. Stress falls on the last stem syllable of most words.

Several Iranian names with their pronunciation are listed below.		Listen to the audio file and write the pronunciation for each name. Divide the words according to their syllables, like the examples to the left.	
Written Form	Pronunciation	Written Form	Pronunciation
Afshin	af-shin	**Sanaz**	
Kasra	kas-râ	**Farangis**	
Kaveh	kâ-ve	**Amirali**	
Arzhang	ar-zhang	**Alireza**	
Bahman	bah-man	**Fatemeh**	
Bardia	bar-diyâ	**Elnaz**	
Behrang	beh-rang	**Hasan**	
Bozorgmehr	bo-zorg-mehr	**Ehsan**	
Kamiar	kam-yâr	**Masud**	

Classroom Activities   فعالیت‌های پیشنهادی در کلاس

۱. دوست یابی سریع

Watch the following video in class and try to guess what it's about:

http://www.youtube.com/watch?v=RY2UEdxQTNE

Now, arrange your chairs in two rows so that you are facing one other person. Mimic what you've seen in the video and have a short converstion with your partner. Make sure you use the greetings that you've learned in the short conversations. If you like your partner, ask him or her for a phone number. After one minute, row one will move to the right, and row two will remain. Have another short converastion and repeat until you have spoken with all the people in the other row!

2. کامران می‌گه

At home, use the audio file to learn the following commands.

look	negâh konid
listen	gush konid
read	bekhunid
write	benevisid
see	bebinid
work	kâr konid
say	begid

In class, play a variation of the game "Simon Says!", "Kamran mige," which means "Kamran says." To begin, one student will stand in front of the class and all of the other students will stand up. The person who is it will give commands to the class and you must act out the command when it is preceeded by "Kamran mige..." If s/he does not say "Kamran mige..." and you act out the command then you are out and must sit down. You are also out if you do not know the command and cannot act it out! Once everyone but one person has been elimanated, a winner is crowned! The winner of the previous round plays "Kamran" in the new round. Continue playing until everyone has been it.

3. **Name Game**: Use the Grammar Note on Iranian names to make up an Iranian name for yourself. Form a circle with your classmates. The first person in the circle should introduce him/herself using the Iranian name that s/he picked and then must ask the next person in the circle what his/her name is. The next person says, "My name is...," and then introduces the first person before asking the next person what his/her name is. The next person must introduce him/herself and say the names of all the people who came before.

درس دوم
UNIT 2

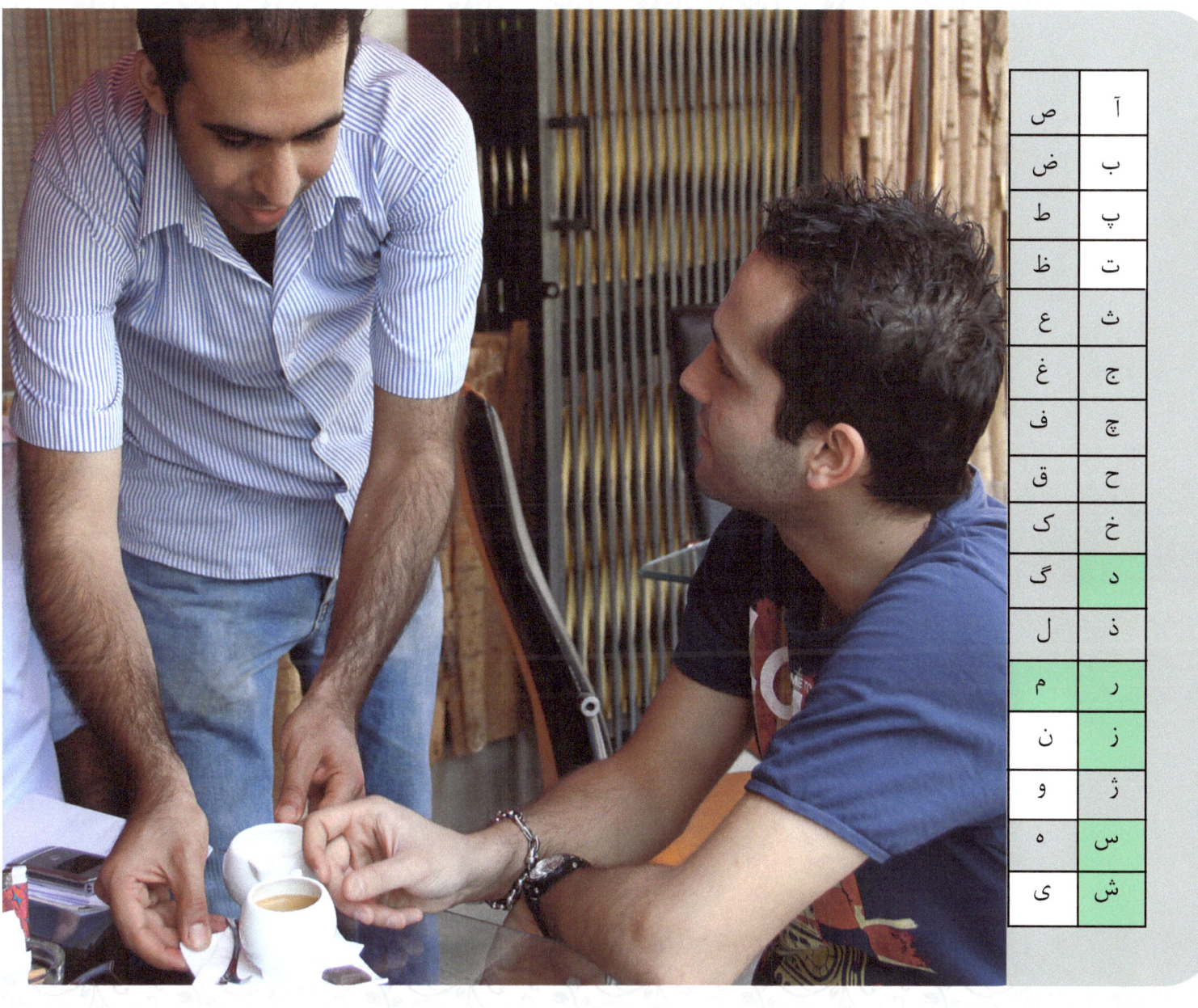

خیلی ممنون — Thank you!

Cultural Note   یادداشت فرهنگی

Greetings 2   سلام و احوالپرسی ۲

ممنونم [mamnunam] is the shortest word to give thanks to someone. It is also one response to «حال شما چطوره؟» [hâl-e shomâ chetore?], and it shows your respect to the person who greets you. ممنونم [mamnunam] is usually followed by other phrases such as قربان شما [qorbân-e shomâ] or ارادتمندم [erâdatmandam]. These phrases, which carry an exaggerated meaning, are part of a system of politeness in Iranian culture called taarof. These words and phrases are used in conversations to show the warmth of people's relationships and to indicate friendliness in daily greetings. These greetings are often used with a smiling face and humble gestures (i.e. placing one's right hand on the chest and bending forward slightly).

Short Conversations   گفتگوهای کوتاه

In class, listen to the audio files and transcribe the conversations. At home repeat what you hear several times and try to follow the rhythm. During the next class time, you will work with a classmate to create a scenario that uses these expressions.

متن فارسی این گفتگوها در انتهای کتاب نوشته شده است.

....

....

....
....
....

....

....

....

...د...	... ر ...	...ز...	...س...س...	...ش.ش...	...م...م...	...ا...اِ...	ه...ه....

In this unit, you will be introduced to seven more letters and sounds of the Persian alphabe t.

Part 1: *dâl* /d/ ____د____

دود	پِدر	باد

1. Listen to the audio file for د *dâl*.

This consonant is pronounced like a clear, frontal /d/ in English, as in the word "dentist" (not like the /d/ sound in "puddle"). Pay close attention to your pronunciation of medial and final د, making sure to pronounce a crisp d sound. The letter د does not connect to any letter that follows it.

2. Watch the video and follow the instructions.

د ....

3-1. Watch the video and write the following words.

دانا .... باد .... بَد .... آبادان ....

3-2. Watch the video and write the following words.

بود .... دود ....

5. Circle the letter د in the following text. Report to your instructor how many د you identified in the text.

4. Listen and check when you hear the /d/ sound in the word.

☐ ۱.
☐ ۲.
☐ ۳.
☐ ۴.
☐ ۵.

7. Connect the letters to form words.	6. Listen and write the words you hear.

۱. ب + ا + د + ی ....

۲. ب + ی + د + ا + د ....

۳. بَ + د + ی ....

۴. آ + ب + ا + د + ی ....

۵. ب + و + دَ + ن ....

۶. ب + د + و + ی ....

۷. دَ + ن + د + ا + ن ....

۱. ....

۲. ....

۳. ....

۴. ....

۵. ....

Part 2: re /r/ ر

رود	برادر	پسر

1. Listen to the audio file for ر re.

This sound is similar to the Spanish or Italian /r/, sometimes called a flap. You already know how to make this sound. It is similar to the sound American English speakers make when saying "gotta" as in "gotta go." Say "gotta" several times in a row very quickly and pay attention to what your tongue is doing. You should feel it flapping against the roof of your mouth behind your teeth. Now pronounce the sound alone. Another good exercise is to practice making a whirring sound: rrrrrrrrrr. Do these exercises daily until you have mastered this sound. This letter is a nonconnector, meaning it does not connect to any letters following it.

2. Watch the video and follow the instructions. Note that the character is slightly different when typewritten than when handwritten.

ر ....

3. Watch the video and write the following words.

دَر .... داراب .... بَر ....

تَبَر .... دیر .... پیر ....

اُروپا .... دَرد .... نَدارَد ....

4. Listen and check when you hear the /r/ sound in the word.

□ ۱. □ ۲. □ ۳. □ ۴. □ ۵.

5. Circle the letter ر in the following text. Report to your instructor how many ر you identified in the text.

سرمقاله / اطلاعات، طراح و طراحی اطلاعات
نظر / طراحی اطلاعات
طراح معاصر ایرانی / فرهاد در سرزمین عجایب
پروژه / علائم و نشانه‌های راه‌آهن شهری تهران و حومه
طراحی امروز / کاتولوگ تری ـ کنترل شده / نشده
روبه‌رو / رابرت اپلتون، ورتکس
مرجع / اسکار رابرت بلچمن ـ خطوط ساخت انسان

نشریه‌ی طراحی گرافیک ایران
شماره‌ی بیست‌وسوم، پاییز ۱۳۸۹
ویژه‌ی طراحی اطلاعات
بهای تک شماره ۷۹۰۰ تومان

NESHAN 23, Information Design
The Iranian Graphic Design Magazine
Autumn 2010

6. Listen and write the words you hear.

۱. ۲. ۳. ۴. ۵.

7. Connect the letter to form words and read them.

۱. د + ی + و + ا + ن   ....

۲. دُ + بِ + ی   ....

۳. دَ + ن + د + ا + ن   ....

۴. ب + و + دَ + ن   ....

۵. بَ + دَ + ن   ....

۶. پِ + ی + د + ا   ....

8. In class, read aloud the following words with your partner.

۱. باران   ۲. اَبرو   ۳. رادار   ۴. پِدَر   ۵. بار   ۶. رو   ۷. ایران

۸. نَداری   ۹. روبِرو   ۱۰. بَردار   ۱۱. دارَد   ۱۲. بُردید   ۱۳. تایِر   ۱۴. نَدارید

۱۵. دُوران   ۱۶. سیر   ۱۷. پوران   ۱۸. بُرد

Part 3: ze /z/ ــز

| زود | بزرگ | دیروز |

1. Listen to the audio file for ز ze.

This consonant corresponds to the English sound /z/ in "zebra." The letter ز is a nonconnector and has the same shape as ر except that it takes one dot above.

2. Watch the video and follow the instructions.

ز ....

3. Watch the video and write the following words.

زود .... زَنبور ....

بازار .... بُز ....

روز .... زَن ....

4. Listen and check when you hear /z/ sound in the word.

١. ☐   ٢. ☐   ٣. ☐   ۴. ☐   ۵. ☐

5. Circle the letter ز in the following text. Report to your instructor how many ز you identified in the text.

حکایت

مردم‌آزاری را حکایت کنند که سنگی بر سر صالحی زد. درویش را مجال انتقام نبود، سنگ را نگاه همی‌داشت تا زمانی که ملک را بر آن لشکری خشم آمد و در چاه کرد. درویش اندر آمد و سنگ در سرش کوفت. گفتا تو کیستی و مرا این سنگ چرا زدی؟ گفت من فلانم و این همان سنگ است که در فلان تاریخ بر سر من زدی. گفت چندین روزگار کجا بودی؟ گفت از جاهت اندیشه همی‌کردم، اکنون که در چاهت دیدم فرصت غنیمت دانستم.

ناسزایی را که بینی بختیار

6. Listen and write the words you hear.

١.   ٢.   ٣.   ۴.   ۵.

۶.   ٧.   ٨.   ٩.   ١٠.

ستاره	بیست	دیس	فارس

Part 4: sin /s/ ‌س‌ ـسـ ـس

1. Listen to the audio file for س sin.

This letter is called *sin* and it corresponds to the English "s" as in the word "seen." Remember that English "s" represents several different sounds, the most common of which is /z/ (like "easy" or plural ending, as in "dogs" or "bugs"). Persian س on the other hand, always retains the soft /s/ sound as in "song."

2. Watch the video and follow the instructions.

س .... سه

3. Watch the video and write the following words.

آسیا .... سَبز

خیس .... سَر

پارسی .... نارسیس

نَسرین .... بِسیار

پِسَر .... بیست

4. Listen and check when you hear the /s/ sound in the word.

☐ ۵. ☐ ۴. ☐ ۳. ☐ ۲. ☐ ۱.

PERSIAN OF IRAN TODAY

5. Circle the letter س in the following text. Report to your instructor how many س you identified in the text.

انسانی در قلمروِ شگفت زده‌ی نگاهِ من
در قلمروِ شگفت زده‌ی دستانِ پرستنده‌ام.
انسانی با همه‌ی ابعادش ــ فارغ از نزدیکی و بُعد
که دستخوشِ زوایای نگاه نمی‌شود.

با طبیعتِ همه‌گانه بیگانه‌یی
که بیننده را
از سلامتِ نگاهِ خویش

آی عشق آی عشق چهره‌ی آبی‌ات پیدا نیست.

6. Listen and write the words you hear.

۱.   ۲.

۳.   ۴.

۵.   ۶.

۷.   ۸.

۹.   ۱۰.

7. Connect the letters to form words. Make sure your answers fit on the line provided.

۱. وَ + ز + ی + ن   ....

۲. ر + و + س   ....

۳. و + ی + ز + ی + ت   ....

۴. پ + ا + ر + ی + س   ....

۵. ی + ز + د + ا + ن   ....

۶. س + ی + م + ا   ....

۷. آ + ز + ا + د + ی   ....

8. Listen to the following words. Write in the missing letter or letters and rewrite the completed words on a separate piece of paper.

۳. رستو____ان	۲. سان____ور	۱. دُ____د
۶. پُ____ز	۵. ویرو____	۴. پَری____
۹. سو____یس	۸. دوز____	۷. ____ودا
۱۲. ز____پ	۱۱. س____نا	۱۰. ____وز
۱۵. دی____ی	۱۴. ی____س	۱۳. بو____تان
۱۸. تابِ____تان	۱۷. ر____ز	۱۶. تنی____

9. Read the following words aloud with your partner.

۴. زیاد	۳. سینا	۲. پَریروز	۱. دیروز
۸. زِبر	۷. پارسیان	۶. زیر	۵. آسان
۱۲. زور	۱۱. سی	۱۰. رُز	۹. آسیب
۱۶. پاییز	۱۵. ساناز	۱۴. بِدوز	۱۳. سوپ
۲۰. آستین	۱۹. دیس	۱۸. نَدوز	۱۷. تِنیس

شربت	بیشتر	ریش	موش

ـــشـــش ش **Part 5: shin /sh/**

1. Listen to the audio file for ش shin

The letter shin corresponds to the sound sh in shoe. It is written exactly like س, but with three dots above it in an upside-down v-shape.

2. Watch the video and follow the instructions.

ش.....ش...

3. Watch the video and write the following words. You'll notice that three words have a letter you don't recognize. Try writing these words like you see in the video and you will learn more about this letter in the next part.

شاد .... رِشادَت .... شیرین ....

ریش .... شور .... موش ....

دَرویش .... شُش .... شُد ....

مَشوِرَت .... پشتو .... امشَب ....

4. Listen and check when you hear the /sh/ sound in the word or phrase.

☐ ۱.   ☐ ۲.   ☐ ۳.   ☐ ۴.   ☐ ۵.

5. Circle the letter ش in the following text. Report to your instructor how many ش you identified in the text.

بهرام صادقی

سنگر و قمقمه‌های خالی

دو قدم این ور خط   احمد پوری

فرشته‌ها بوی پرتقال می‌دهند

حسن بنی عامری

6. Listen and write the words you hear.

١.   ٢.   ٣.   ۴.   ۵.

۶.   ٧.   ٨.   ٩.   ١٠.

Part 6: *mim* /m/ ‎ـمـ‎ | مرد | بیمار | بیم | شام |

1. Listen to the audio file for م *mim*.

The pronunciation of the letter *mim* corresponds to the English "m" as in "may."

2. Watch the video and follow the instructions.

م..م..

3. Watch the video and write the following words.

ماست...............................موش...............................شام...............................

روم...............................مَرد...............................اِسم...............................

سَمت...............................کَمَر...............................سامان...............................

4. Listen and check when you hear the /m/ sound in the word.

☐ ١.   ☐ ٢.   ☐ ٣.   ☐ ۴.   ☐ ۵.

35 PERSIAN OF IRAN TODAY

5. Circle the letter م in the following text. Report to your instructor how many م you identified in the text.

ای فرستاده سلامم به سلامت باشی
غم آن نیست که قادر به غرامت باشی

گل که دل زنده کند بوی وفایی دارد
تو مگر صاحبِ اعجاز وکرامت باشی

خانهٔ دل نه چنان ریخته از هم که دراو
سر فرود آری ومایل به اقامت باشی

6. Listen and write the words you hear.

۱. ۲. ۳. ۴. ۵.

۶. ۷. ۸. ۹. ۱۰.

Part 7: e âkhar /e/ ___ﻪ___ﻩ___

| سه | کوره | شانه |

1. Listen to the audio file. The first word you hear is *emruz*, which starts with the /e/ sound (*zir*). This word is not included in the box above, but we have included it to let you know that the sound /e/ which starts *emruz* is represented by a different letter when it comes at the end of the word.

This letter, called *he*, has two functions in Persian, the first of which you will learn now. With this first function, *he* represents the vowel sound /e/ in *Desirée*. but only when it comes at the very end of a word and is preceded by a consonant and not another vowel.

2. Watch the video and follow the instructions.

اِ.............ه............ه.............ُ

3. Watch the video and write the following words.

سه............شَنبه...................

سوریه..................کوره...............شانه...............

4. Listen and check when you hear the /e/ sound in a word that is written with ه.

☐ ۱.   ☐ ۲.   ☐ ۳.   ☐ ۴.   ☐ ۵.

5. Circle the letter ه in the following text. Report to your instructor how many ه you identified in the text.

مجموعه تئاترشهر: خیابان انقلاب- چهار راه ولی عصر- مجموعه تئاترش
تماشاخانه سنگلج: ضلع جنوب شرقی پارک شهر- خیابان بهشت- تلفن
تماشاخانه ایرانشهر: خیابان طالقانی- خیابان شهید موسوی- خانه هنرم

6. Listen and write the words you hear.

۱.   ۲.   ۳.   ۴.   ۵.

۶.   ۷.   ۸.   ۹.   ۱۰.

PERSIAN OF IRAN TODAY

7. Connect the letters to form words.

۱. رَ + و + ش ....

۲. م + ی + و + ه ....

۳. بِ + ش + ا + رَ + ت ....

۴. س + و + ا + ر + ه ....

۵. پ + و + ش + ه ....

۶. اُ + س + ت + ا + د ....

۷. مَ + ر + دُ + م ....

8. Listen to the following words. Fill in the missing letter or letters and rewrite the completed word on a separate piece of paper.

۱. برو___ور   ۲. شا___پو

۳. ___شی___   ۴. ___اشین

۵. ___شـ___ر   ۶. تو___ور

۷. بُـ___ب   ۸. ما___رَ

۹. مِر___ی   ۱۰. آ___ازون

۱۱. ار___نستان ۱۲. مـ___ت

۱۳. مـ___ت   ۱۴. بیمارِ___تان

۱۵. مو___   ۱۶. شـ___دا

۱۷. آ___تی   ۱۸. آبشـ___ر

9. Read the following words aloud with your partner.

۱. شوش   ۲. ریتم   ۳. بُرَنده

۴. مَدرِسه   ۵. ویتامین   ۶. ساده

۷. مَرسوم   ۸. سَواره   ۹. شیمی

۱۰. پیاده   ۱۱. مومیا   ۱۲. شُرشُر

۱۳. داده   ۱۴. میان   ۱۵. شَربَت

۱۶. شَرمَنده ۱۷. موز   ۱۸. تَمیز

۱۹. شیشه   ۲۰. مادَر   ۲۱. زِمِستان

10. Listen to the audio file and mark the word you hear.

۱	O بود O بَد	۷	O باد O بَد
۲	O پور O پُر	۸	O دَد O داد
۳	O نار O نَر	۹	O دار O دَر
۴	O شور O شُر	۱۰	O سیر O سر
۵	O دار O دَر	۱۱	O سور O سُر
۶	O تار O تَر	۱۲	O دور O دُر

واژگان Vocabulary

1. Listen to the following words and memorize them. The spoken variations are included in parentheses.

English	Example	Word
I	مَن؟	۱. مَن
you (plural or respectful singular)	شما؟	۲. شُما
friend / my friend	این دوستِ من اَست. (این دوستِ منه.)	۳. دوست/دوستَم
I have / I do not have	من نان ندارم. (من نون ندارم.)	۴. دارَم/ نَدارَم
you have / you do not have	شما نان دارید؟ (شما نون دارین؟)	۵. دارید/ نَدارید
I like	نان دوست دارید؟ (نون دوست دارین؟)	۶. دوست دارَم
I do not like	من نان دوست ندارم؟! (من نون دوست ندارم؟!)	۷. دوست نَدارَم
you like	نان دوست ندارید؟ (نون دوست ندارین؟)	۸. دوست دارید
you do not like	شما نان دوست ندارید؟ (شما نون دوست ندارین؟)	۹. دوست نَدارید
brother	من برادر ندارم.	۱۰. بَرادَر
sport, exercise	ورزش دوست ندارید؟ (ورزش دوست ندارین؟)	۱۱. وَرزِش
sweets, dessert	شما شیرینی دوست دارید؟ (شما شیرینی دوست دارین)	۱۲. شیرینی
ice cream	من بستنی دوست دارم.	۱۳. بَستَنی
mother	او مادر من است (اون مادر منه.)	۱۴. مادَر
father	او پدر شما است. (اون پدر شماست.)	۱۵. پِدَر
he, she	او برادر من است. (اون برادر منه)	۱۶. او (اون)
he, she (polite)	ایشون پدر شما است . (ایشون پدر شماست.)	۱۷. ایشان (ایشون)
thirsty	مادر من تشنه است. (مادر من تشنهست)	۱۸. تِشنه
and	من بستنی و شیرینی دوست دارم.	۱۹. وَ
pomegranate	من انار دوست دارم.	۲۰. اَنار
apple	سیب و انار دوست دارم.	۲۱. سیب
almond	بادام دوست دارید؟ (بادوم دوست دارین؟)	۲۲. بادام
but	سیب دوست ندارم، امّا انار دوست دارم.	۲۳. امّا
tennis	ورزش دوست ندارم، اما تنیس دوست دارم.	۲۴. تنیس
soup	این سوپ بادام دارد. (این سوپ بادوم داره.)	۲۵. سوپ

2. Listen to the audio file again. Based on what you hear, write the vowel on the example sentences. Now listen to the next audio file. Write the sentences you hear and translate them to English.

Listening Comprehension  درک شنیدار

1. Watch Video 1 and transcribe the conversation you hear.

- ……………………………………………………………………
- ……………………………………………………………………
- ……………………………………………………………………
- ……………………………………………………………………
- ……………………………………………………………………
- ……………………………………………………………………

2. Watch Video 2 and answer the following questions in Persian.

1. What do Shayli's parents like?
2. Where do you think they live?
3. How many hours do they exercise every day?
4. Does Shayliy like to exercise?
5. What does she like?
6. What does she say before she drinks the water?

Start making flash cards for each word you learn. Write the word in Persian on one side. On the other side, write the translation and create a sentence using the word.

Grammar Note — یادداشت دستوری

Sentence Structure or Word Order

The simplest sentence structure in Persian is subject + verb. The verb is placed at the end of the sentence.

Persian Sentence	من man	می‌روم miravam
English Equivalent	I	go
Function in Sentence	subject	verb

In English sentences, the subject comes first, followed by the verb and then the object. This is often referred to as Subject-Verb-Object (SVO) word order. Word order in Persian is slightly different in that it follows SOV word order, with the verb usually coming at the end of the sentence. Look at the examples below:

این	دوستم	است
this	my friend	is

The following sentence is more complex. Read it from right to left.

من	امروز	کتابم را	به دوستم	می‌دهم
I	today	my book	to my friend	give
subject	adverb	direct object	object of preposition	verb

Now write sentences with each set of the words.

۱. دارید . شُما . برادر

۲. دوست دارد . بَرادَرم . بستنی

۳. او . است . برادرم

۴. او . است . دوست . شما

۵. من . ندارم. برادر

41 PERSIAN OF IRAN TODAY

Subject Pronouns ضمیر فاعلی

So far you've seen several of the personal pronouns in class. Study the chart below and memorize the pronouns and their spellings.

we	ما	I	مَن
you (singular polite/plural)	شُما	you (just for close friends)	تو
they	آنها (اونا)	he/she he/she (polite) it	او (اون) ایشان (ایشون) آن (اون)

- The spoken variations are in parentheses.
- تو is used for close friends, sometimes family members, when addressing God, and also for insults.
- Use ایشان or او, and use اون for "he" or "she" when you speak rather than ایشان or او, and use اون for "it."

Infinitive /masdar/ مصدر

Infinitive in English is the basic form of a verb, without an inflection binding it to a particular subject or tense (e.g., I am going <u>to see</u> him, or let me <u>see</u>.) Infinitive is called مصدر "masdar" in Persian. The infinitive in Persian is normally equated with the English infinitive, but it is more like the English gerund, that is, a verb in -ing when it does not represent a progressive form as in "Reading is good": خواندن کار خوبی است xāndan kār-e xubi ast. Therefore, in Persian an infinitive also functions as a gerund.

To Have (Present Tense) فعل داشتن (زمان حال)

In Persian, the verb "to have" has a present-tense stem دار. We add endings to that stem to conjugate the verb for different pronouns. Look at the chart below; notice that the first three letters are the same for each conjugation. Only the last letter or two letters differ.

Present-tense stem is called **"bon-e haal"** in Persian.

داشتن - دار

داریم	ما	دارَم	من
دارید (دارین)	شما	دارَی	تو
دارَند (دارن)	آنها (اونا)	دارَد (داره) دارَند (دارن)	او (اون) ایشون

Verb Endings

Look at the chart on the previous page. Determine what letter or letters we put at the end of the present-tense stem دار to indicate a particular person. Use that information to complete the chart below. Memorize these endings. We will use them again and again to conjugate verbs.

Verb Ending Spoken	Verb Ending Written	Pronoun ضمیر فاعلی
		من
		تو
		او (اون)/ ایشان (ایشون)
		ما
		شما
		آنها (اونا)

Practice: Complete the following sentences with the appropriate form of the verb "to have."

ما بستنی ....

من و تو شیرینی ....

ما و شما خواهر ....

من و او بستنی ....

من و تو و او بادام ....

من و شما تنیس ....

شما و آنها اَنار ....

Negating "to have"

You have already learned how to say "I do not have" and "you do not have." Look at the chart below.

نَدارم	دارم
نَدارید	دارید

Can you see the difference between the two columns? What changes are marking negation? Try filling in the chart below using the information you have just discovered.

		داشتن - دار
ندارم		من
	داری	تو
	دارد	او
	داریم	ما
ندارید		شما
	دارند	آنها

Fill in the blank with the appropriate form of داشتن (to have). You can write about the following things:

پیتزا، بستنی، شیرینی، برادر، سوپ، نان، شامپو، ماشین، پودر، بادام، انار، ورزش، سیب، تنیس

You can also add دوست to داشتن to write about what the following people like or dislike.

من و تو ....
من و او ....
من و آنها ....
من و شما ....
او و شما ....
شما و او ....
او و ما ....
او و آنها ....
او و تو ....
تو و او ....

تو و آنها ....
تو و من ....
من و تو ....
ما و تو ....
ما و او ....
ما و آنها ....
ما و شما ....
برادر و پدرم ....
پدر و مادرم ....
پدر دوستم و برادرم ....
ما و آنها و شما ....

1. Choose the best written form for each word.

#		
1	sharmandeh	○ شرمنده ○ شرمند
2	mosalmân	○ مسلمان ○ مسالمان
3	sepâs	○ سپاس ○ سپاس
4	hamedâni	○ هامدانی ○ همدانی
5	âbshâr	○ آبشار ○ آبیشار
6	zemestân	○ زمیستان ○ زمستان
7	berereshte	○ برشته ○ برشت
8	hamishe	○ همشه ○ همیشه
9	emshab	○ ایمشب ○ امشب
10	lârestân	○ لارستن ○ لارستان

2. Write the words in Persian.

1. mosâvât .... ۱.
2. mi-shavad .... ۲.
3. suriye .... ۳.
4. sarâsar .... ۴.
5. barâzande .... ۵.
6. dâyere .... ۶.
7. turân .... ۷.
8. bimârestân .... ۸.
9. marzbân .... ۹.
10. sâmâne .... ۱۰.

3. Write sentences with each word.

۱. شُما ....

۲. بَرادَر ....

۳. دوست ....

۴. وَرزِش ....

۵. تِشنه ....

Match the following vocabulary words with their corresponding picture. Write the appropriate number for each word.

۱. ورزش   ۲. دوست دارم   ۳. بستنی   ۴. تشنه‌ام   ۵. شیرینی   ۶. شما

Writing Exercise نوشتن

Watch Shaily's video again and see how she talks about her family. Write a short paragraph about yourself and your family. What do you like and dislike? What does your family like and dislike?

Speaking Activities حرف زدن

At Home:

Based on the vocabulary and grammar and the videos you have seen, think about how you might ask (andanswer) the following questions.

~ What is you father's name?
~ Do you have a brother?
~ Do you like exercise?
~ Does you mother like ice cream?
~ Do you like sweets?
~ Does your father like soup?

> Look at the following examples with translations. Can you tell what happens to word order when asking questions in Persian?
>
> 1. Your brother likes ice cream.
> 2. Does your brother like ice cream?
>
> ۱. بَرادَرتان بستنی دوست دارند.
> ۲. بَرادَرتان بستنی دوست دارند؟

In Class:

Now, practice with your classmates. Ask your neighbors the questions above. Pay attention to what they say, because your instructor may ask you to report what you've learned to the class.

Classroom Activities فعالیت‌های پیشنهادی در کلاس

1. **Tit-for-Tat, This-and-That**: Review the words on page 32. Your instructor will provide you with index cards with pictures on them. Each person will get four index cards. Work with partner. You should find out what is on his/her index cards by asking "What is that?" and replying "This is..."

2. **Story Wars**: Review the vocabulary on page 53. Your instructor will divide the class into two groups. Each group will be given a short list of words (11 words). Work together to write a short story that incorporates all of the words. After 15 minutes, you must share your story with the class. The instructor will help you pick the best story!

3. **I Scream, You Scream, We all Scream for Ice Cream**: Your instructor will give you a set of index cards with words or pictures from the vocabulary. Using only Persian, you will work with a partner and together you must determine which words you both have, and which words are different.

برای استاد: در این بازی دو نفره به هر دانشجو ۵ کارت داده می‌شود. هر گروه ۳ کارت مشابه و دو کارت متفاوت دارند. دانشجوها باید کارت‌های مشابه‌شان را بیابند. مثال:

من انار دارم. تو انار داری؟
من انار دارم! ... ما انار داریم!

درس سوم
UNIT 3

ص	آ
ض	ب
ط	پ
ظ	ت
ع	ث
غ	ج
ف	چ
ق	ح
ک	خ
گ	د
ل	ذ
م	ر
ن	ز
و	ژ
ه	س
ی	ش

I am Asadi.   اسدی هستم.

Cultural Note   یادداشت فرهنگی

Introductions   معرفی کردن

Using just your last name is a common way to introduce yourself to someone whom you have not met before. Usually, men introduce themselves and offer to shake hands when they meet other men. However, it is not appropriate for a man and a woman to shake hands when introducing themselves in public places, such as an office or university. Avoiding eye contact between men and women as they introduce themselves is also considered as a modest and respectful gesture. In less formal settings, like a family gathering or a friend's party, it is common among non-religious men and women to shake hands while introducing themselves. In such situations, women are usually responsible for initiating the handshake to indicate they are comfortable doing so.

Short Conversations   گفتگوهای کوتاه

In class, listen to the audio files, repeat what you hear and try to fill in the blanks and transcribe the sentences. At home repeat what you hear several times and try to follow the rhythm. Write a sentence in Persian about each conversation you hear. During the next class time, you will work with a classmate to create a scenario that uses these expressions.

- سلام، من مهدی هستم، ....
- سلام، خیلی خوشوقتم. من .... هستم.
- خیلی خوشوقتم.

....

....

....

١. ....

- سلام، .... هستم.
- سلام، مساوات .... خیلی خوشوقتم.
- خوشوقتم از آشناییتون.

....

....

....

١. ....

PERSIAN OF IRAN TODAY

۱. سلام مرجان، این مریمه. مریم این مرجانه.
. سلام، مریم خوشوقتم.
. سلام، حالتون چه‌طوره؟
. خوبم، متشکرم.

....
....
....
....
....

| ...ج..ج... | ...ل...ل... | ...ه..ه...ه...ه... |

In this unit you will learn two more Persian consonants and the second use of the letter ه.

Part 1: jim /j/ ‎‏ـج‌ـ‎ ‏ج‎

| جلد | مجّانی | هویج | موج |

1. Listen to the audio file for ج jim.

The letter *jim* is pronounced like *j* in *jack*. Pay close attention to how this letter is written. You will learn three more letters that are written similarly in future units.

2. Watch the video and follow the instructions.

ج ج ....

3. Watch the video and write the following words.

جَشن .... پَنجَره .... مُجاوِر ....

بُرج .... جوجه .... بِرنج ....

4. Listen and check when you hear the /j/ sound in the word.

۱. ☐   ۲. ☐   ۳. ☐   ۴. ☐   ۵. ☐

5. Circle the letter ج in the following text. Report to your instructor how many ج you identified in the text.

6. Listen and write the words you hear.

۱.   ۲.   ۳.   ۴.   ۵.

۶.   ۷.   ۸.   ۹.   ۱۰.

Part 2: lâm /l/ _ل‍__ل‍_

| لادن | شی‍لی | پُل | دِل |

1. Listen to the audio file for ل lâm.

This letter represents the sound of the Spanish or French "l," that is, a frontal "l" in which the front part of the tongue is against the back of the teeth, and the tongue is high in the mouth. Americans tend to pronounce "l" with the tongue farther back and lower down in the mouth, resulting in a more emphatic sound than the Persian ل. To pronounce Persian ل, hold the tip of your tongue against the back of your teeth at the roof of your mouth and keep your tongue as high and as far forward as you can.

2. Watch the video and follow the instructions.

ل .... لا ....

3. Watch the video and write the following words.

لوله .... لِیلا ....

سومالی .... شُمال ....

مَلَوان .... مُسَلمان ....

سلام .... سلامتی ....

لالایی ....

4. Listen and check when you hear the /l/ sound in the word.

۱. ☐   ۲. ☐   ۳. ☐   ۴. ☐   ۵. ☐

5. Circle the letter ل in the following texts. Report to your instructor how many ل you identified in the text.

برف، بلوز، شلوار

اگر دنبال لباس مهمانی زمستانه می‌گردید، این صفحات به شما کمک خواهند کرد

مهمانی رفتن که سرما و گرما ندارد. نمی‌توانید به خاطر سرما بنشینید توی خانه و تمام دعوت‌ها را رد کنید. برای مهمانی رفتن با خیال راحت، قبل از هر کاری باید لباس مناسب تهیه کنید. انتخاب لباس مناسب مهمانی در این فصل قواعد خودش را دارد. نه می‌توان با لباس‌های تابستانه رفت مهمانی نه می‌توان لباس‌های خیلی گرم پوشید. چون معمولاً درون خانه‌ها گرم است، اگر لباس شما یک پلیور ضخیم باشد اذیت خواهید شد. پس باید تعادلی بین این دو برقرار کنید. امسال بلوزهای بافتنی را زیاد می‌توانید در بازار پیدا کنید. تونیک هم انتخاب خوبی برای این فصل است. اکثر شلوارهای بازار پاچه گشاد هستند که نمی‌توان آنها را با کفش‌های بوت بلند پوشید. برای اینکه راحت‌تر بتوانید انتخاب کنید؛ پیشنهادهای زندگی ایده‌آل را برای داشتن بهترین ظاهر زمستانی بخوانید.

6. Listen and write the words you hear.

۱. ۲. ۳. ۴. ۵.

۶. ۷. ۸. ۹. ۱۰.

Part 3: he /h/ ‎ه‎ ‎ه‎ ‎ه‎ ‎ه‎

همان	بهتر	ماه	نه

1. Listen to the audio file for ه he.

You have already learned that in specific circumstances, ه represents the /e/ sound in bet. In other positions, this letter represents the sound of English /h/ in house. Unlike the English "h," which can be silent, as in the word hour, ه is always pronounced, unless it is at the end of the word. Watch the video to see how this letter's shape is different when typed vs. handwritten, like "a" in English.

Remember: When ه comes at the end of the word and is immediately preceded by a consonant and no vowel sound, it makes an /e/ sound. However if it is at the end of a word and is preceded by a written or unwritten vowel, then it makes an /h/ sound.

2. Watch the video and follow the instructions.

ه .... ه ....

ه .... ه ....

3. Watch the video and write the following words.

هَستَم .... شَهر ....

مَشهور .... بَه بَه ....

ماه .... پَناه ....

PERSIAN OF IRAN TODAY

4. Listen and check when you hear the /h/ sound in the word.

☐ ۵.   ☐ ۴.   ☐ ۳.   ☐ ۲.   ☐ ۱.

5. Circle the letter ل in the following text. Report to your instructor how many ل you identified in the text.

مجموعه تئاترشهر: خیابان انقلاب - چهار راه ولی عصر - مجموعه تئاترشهر
تماشاخانه سنگلج: ضلع جنوب شرقی پارک شهر - خیابان بهشت - تلفن: ۴
تماشاخانه ایرانشهر: خیابان طالقانی - خیابان شهید موسوی - خانه هنرمندان

6. Listen and write the words you hear.

۵.   ۴.   ۳.   ۲.   ۱.

۱۰.   ۹.   ۸.   ۷.   ۶.

Extra Practice: Read the words below. Determine whether the ه in each word represents a /h/ sound or an /e/ sound. Explain why.

Word	/ h /	/e /	Explanation
۱. پنج شَنبه			
۲. ماه			
۳. بَه بَه			
۴. میوه			
۵. تَوَجُّه			
۶. به			

7. Connect the letters to form words and read them aloud.

۱. جُ + م + ه + و + ر + ی ....
۲. مَ + ج + لِ + س ....
۳. س + ا + ل + ا + د ....
۴. هَ + م + س + ا + ی + ه ....
۵. شَ + ه + ر + ی + وَ + ر ....
۶. اُ + س + ت + ا + د ....
۷. و + ا + ن + ی + ل ....

8. Listen to the following words. Fill in the missing letter(s) for each word, and then write the complete word on a separate piece of paper.

۲. ه___ات
۱. بود__ه
۴. پن___ان
۳. ا__ناس
۶. ش___ادت
۵. نج___ب
۸. ن___اد
۷. ج__سه
۱۰. هست__م
۹. تبدی__
۱۲. ج__د
۱۱. __هام
۱۴. ه__تند
۱۳. __مسر
۱۵. اس__ اندارد

9. Read the following words aloud with your partner.

۱. جاز ۲. مالاریا
۳. جیپ ۴. هُتِل
۵. دانشجو ۶. ویلا
۷. مُجاوَرَت ۸. وانیل
۹. مَجنون ۱۰. شال
۱۱. جِنس ۱۲. سالاد
۱۳. جَشن ۱۴. مُدِل
۱۵. جانوَر ۱۶. مَجلِس
۱۷. سَمبُل ۱۸. لانه
۱۹. میلیون ۲۰. مِهمان
۲۱. ایتالیا ۲۲. آلمان
۲۳. لیمو ۲۴. رَها

10. Listen to the audio file and mark the word you hear.

۱	بِده بَله		۷	پُل پُر
۲	کَلَم کَرَم		۸	دله دره
۳	دِلم دِرهم		۹	کولی کوری
۴	لُر دُر		۱۰	سیر سیل
۵	بله بره		۱۱	سوره سوله
۶	سراب سلام		۱۲	لام رام

11. Listen to the audio file and fill in the missing letters for each word, then write the English equivalent.

۱. تـ__ران   ۲. روسـ__ــه   ۳. ار__نستان   ۴. هـ__ـد

۵. __یراز   ۶. استرا__یا   ۷. اتری__   ۸. پورت__ند

۹. سیاتـ__   ۱۰. لـ__ آنجلس   ۱۱. ویرجیـ__یا   ۱۲. مـ__ارستان

۱۳. دهـ__ی   ۱۴. تَبـ__یز   ۱۵. تو__نتو

واژگان Vocabulary

1. Listen to and learn these words. Translate the sentences. The spoken variations have been included in parentheses.

۱. سَلام	سلام، بستنی داری؟ (سلام، بستنی دارین؟)	hello
۲. هستَم	من برادر او هستم. (من برادر اون هستم.)	I am
۳. هستید (هستین)	شما پرستار هستید؟ (شما پرستار هستین؟)	you are
۴. نیستَم	من پدر او نیستم. (من پدر اون نیستم.)	I am not
۵. نیستید (نیستین)	شما پرستار نیستید؟ (شما پرستار نیستین؟)	you are not
۶. دانِشجو	شما دانشجو هستید؟ (شما دانشجوهستین؟)	university student
۷. اُستاد	پدر او استاد است. (پدر او استاده.)	professor
۸. اِسم	اسم من امیر است. (اسم من امیره.)	name
۹. ما	ما تشنه هستیم. (ما تشنه‌مونه.)	we
۱۰. هَستیم	دانشجو هستیم.	we are
۱۱. نیستیم	ما استاد نیستیم.	we are not
۱۲. ایرانی	ما ایرانی هستیم.	Iranian
۱۳. تِهران/ تهرانی	ما تهرانی هستیم. (ما تهرونی هستیم.)	Tehran / from Tehran
۱۴. داری	شیرینی داری؟	you have (for close friends)
۱۵. دارَد	او سه دانشجو دارد. (اون سه تا دانشجو داره.)	he / she has
۱۶. داریم	سوپ داریم؟	we have
۱۷. دارَند	برادر دارند؟ (برادر دارن؟)	he / she has, they have
۱۸. آنها (اونا)	آنها شیرینی دوست ندارند. (اوناشیرینی دوست ندارن.)	they

nurse	من پرستار نیستم.	۱۹. پرستار	
They are from Tehran.	آنها تهرانی هستند. (اونا تهرونی هستن.)	۲۰. هستند	
my mother	مادرم پرستار است. (مادرم پرستاره.)	۲۱. مادرم	
my father	من و پدرم تشنه هستیم.	۲۲. پدرم	
this	این شیرینی است. (این شیرینیه)	۲۳. این	
it, that	آن شیرینی ایرانی است.(اون شیرینی ایرانیه.)	۲۴. آن (اون)	
woman	این زن مادرم است. (این زن مادرمه.)	۲۵. زن	
man	آن مرد ایرانی است. (اون مرد ایرانیه.)	۲۶. مرد	

2. Listen to the audio file again. Based on what you hear, write the vowel on the example sentences.
Now listen to the next audio file. Write the sentences you hear and translate them to English.

Listening Comprehension   درک شنیدار

1. Watch the videos and transcribe the conversation that you hear.

2. Watch the videos and answer the following questions in Persian.

1. What does the first man ask the other?
2. How does the second man answer?

3. What does the first girl ask the other?
4. How does the second girl answer?

3. Watch the videos and answer the following question in Persian.

- What did you learn about Amin? Who is he?
What does he like?

4. Listen to the audio files and answer the following questions. Practice each conversation out loud several times. You will be required to use them in class.

a. Write 2-4 sentences about رامین.
b. Write 2-4 sentences aboiut مرجان.
c. What does مرجان say to end the conversation?

Grammar Note — یادداشت دستوری

The Verb "To Be"

In this lesson, you learned to say "I am" and "you are." Just like the verb "to have," the verb "to be" is conjugated in the present tense based on a stem (هست) and different endings that indicate who or what you're talking about.

The Verb "To Be" — بودن

من	هستَم
تو	هستی
او (اون)	هست/ است (ـه)
ما	هستیم
شما	هستید (هستین)
آنها (اونا)	هستَند (هستن)

Note that you should use شما and ایشون instead of تو and او if you are not talking to (or about) your close friend:

شما استاد فیزیک ما هستید؟
شما مادر این دانشجو هستید؟
ایشون استاد فیزیک ما هستند.
ایشون مادر دوستم هستند.

Look at the chart that starts with "I am a nurse" Complete the other chart starting with "I am thirsty."

من تشنه هستم.		من پرستار هستم.	
تو		تو پرستار هستی.	
او		او پرستار است.	
ما		ما پرستار هستیم.	
شما		شما پرستار هستید.	
آنها		آنها پرستار هستند.	

In unit 7, you will learn about the condensed version (فرم کوتاه) of the present tense "to be". The short form of verb "to be" is the common form in spoken form. These charts show that the Persian verb "to be" has a condensed form in Persian.

من تشنه‌ام.		من پرستارَم.	
توتشنه‌ای.		تو پرستاری.	
او تشنه است.		او پرستار است.	
ما تشنه‌ایم.		ما پرستاریم.	
شماتشنه‌اید.		شما پرستارید.	
آنها تشنه‌اند.		آنها پرستارَند.	

The Verb "To Be"

Negating the verb "to be": You also learned how to say "I am not" and "you are not" in this lesson. The negation of "to be" follows the same rules as the regular conjugation for "to be," except it uses the stem نیست. The third-person singular (he/she/it) is also irregular. Can you guess what it is? Try filling out the following chart.

نبودن

من	نیستَم
تو	نیستی
او (اون)	نیست
ما	نیستیم
شما	نیستید (نیستین)
آنها (اونا)	نیستَند (نیستن)

Some Good News!

First read these sentences:

او برادر ندارد.
او برادر ندارد؟

How are these two sentences different? Correct! The first one is a statement and the second is a question. So the good news is that no change of order is needed to express a question in Persian. How do we know it is a question then? Based on intonation. From now on, pay attention to the sentences you hear. For example, listen to these sentences:

من ایرانی هستم.

شما ایرانی هستید؟

(اون بستنی دوست داره؟)

In class listen to your instructor read the following sentences. You have not heard them before. You probably do not know what they mean. Just listen and put a period at the end of the ones that sound like statements and a question mark at the end of the ones that sound like questions.

کیفم رو از اینجا برمی‌داری

از مدرسه برگشت

دانشگاهش رو دوست داره

درس می‌خونه

کار نمی‌کنه

فردا تعطیله

Grammar Exercises

1. Organize the following sets of words into meaningful sentences.

۱. دانشجو، هستیم، ما ....

۲. هستند، آنها، استاد ....

۳. تشنه، شما، هستید ....

۴. است، مادرم، او ....

۵. سوپ، است، مادرم، امّا، تشنه، پدرم، دوست دارد ....

۶. هستیم، پدرم، تشنه، من، و ....

۷. دوست، پدرم، دارد، بادام ....

2. Negate the sentences you constructed in the exercise above.

۱. ....

۲. ....

۳. ....

۴. ....

۵. ....

۶. ....

۷. ....

3. Translate the sentences from both preceding sections.

1. ....

2. ....

3. ....

4. ....

5. ....

6. ....

7. ....

4. Match the following vocabulary words with a corresponding picture and write 4 sentences with the words.

١. ....

٢. ....

٣. ....

٤. ....

١. پرستار ٢. دانشجو ٣. استاد ٤. سلام

Writing Exercise — نوشتن

Use what you have learned to write 10 sentences about you, and your family and friends.

Speaking Activities — حرف زدن

Watch Video 2 with your instructor in class. You will learn how to say what you are and what you are not. After the video clip, practice this structure with your classmates. Ask them if:

~ they are students, professors, mothers, fathers, Iranians, etc.
~ their parents, brothers, professors, or friends are Iranian.
~ their name is Iranian.

In order to practice the plural, work in small groups and ask several classmates at once.

Classroom Activities — فعالیت‌های پیشنهادی برای کلاس

Scavenger Hunt: Use the list below to complete a scavenger hunt in class. You should ask your classmates in Persian if they match the description on the list. If they do, write their name next to the appropriate description. You can only write each person's name down twice.

Someone whose father is Iranian ....
Someone whose brother's name is Iranian ....
Someone whose father's friend is a student ....
Someone who likes Iranian ice cream ....
Someone who is thirsty ....
Someone whose father is Iranian but whose mother is not Iranian ....
Someone who doesn't like exercise but likes tennis..
Someone who likes sweets but does not like exercise ....
Someone who likes soup and almonds..

درس چهارم
UNIT 4

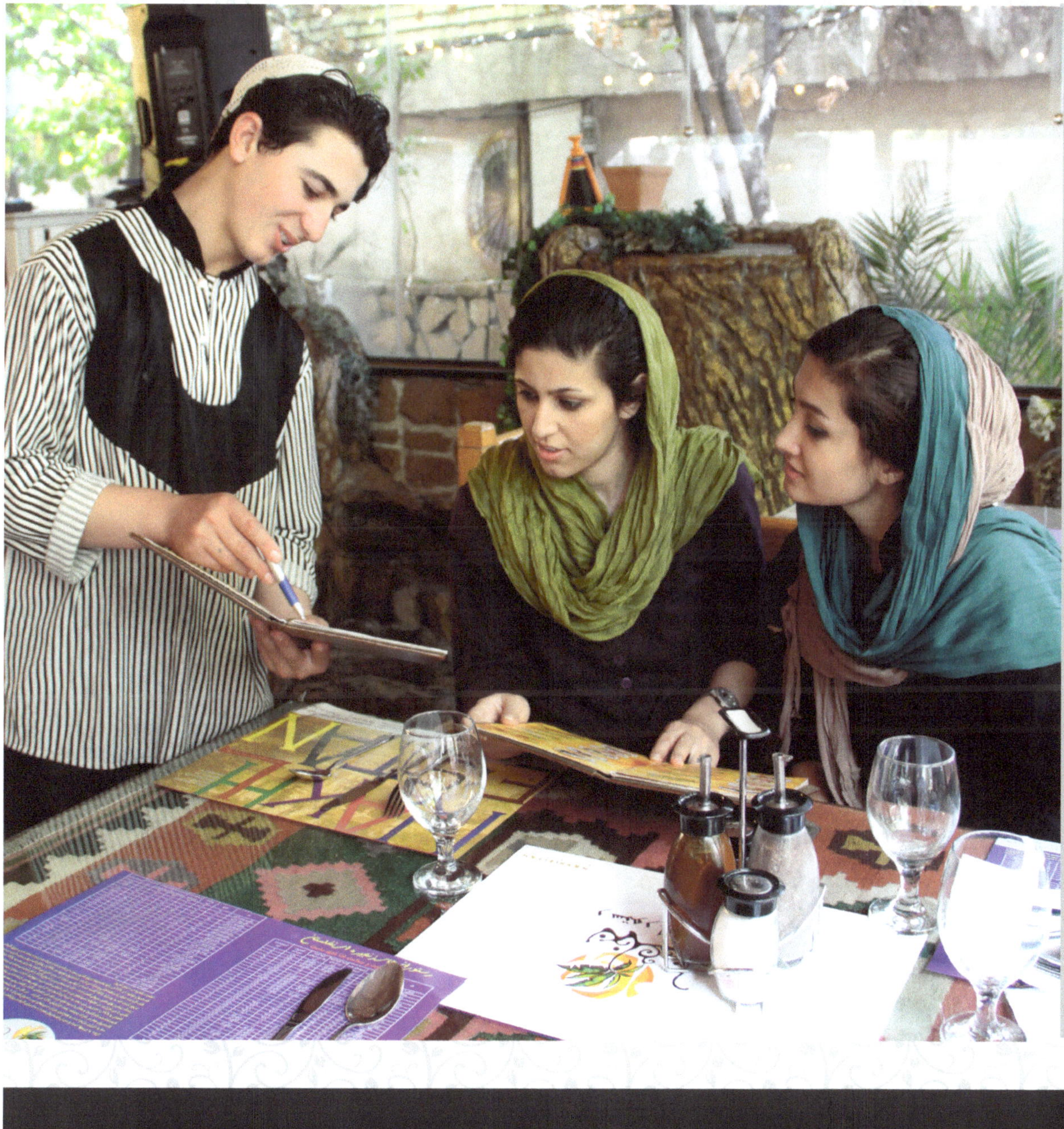

ص	آ
ض	ب
ط	پ
ظ	ت
ع	ث
غ	ج
ف	چ
ق	ح
ک	خ
گ	د
ل	ذ
م	ر
ن	ز
و	ژ
ه	س
ی	ش

What would you like to drink? نوشیدنی چی میل دارید؟

Cultural Note   یادداشت فرهنگی

غذا   Food

In Iranian culture, family practices are rooted in the preparation and consumption of colorful foods. Persian food is often prepared using a variety of different spices. However, the spiciness of the foods may vary depending on which part of the country the cook is from. Southern food is spicier and hotter; while foods from central Iran are not hot, but still flavorfully seasoned with spices such as cumin and cardamom; and northern meals tend to include far fewer spices and seasoning. Iranian families eat three meals during the day. Lunch is the main dish in Iran and usually takes place at some point between 12:30 and 2:00 PM. This meal usually includes white rice and a kind of meat stew in addition to several side dishes such as salads, fresh herbs, plain yogurt, and radishes or pickled vegetables. Purchasing fresh-baked bread on a daily basis is still a common practice in the everyday life of Iranian families. Usually fresh lavash, barbari, sangak, or taftoon breads are purchased early in the morning to start the day with fresh bread for breakfast. Dinner is commonly served in the late evenings at around 8:30 or 9:00 PM. Unless there is a family gathering, dinner usually features a light dish that has more vegetables and less rice and meat. The contents of dinner may vary according to the season. For example, kookoo کوکو, a kind of Persian soufflé that includes eggs, a vegetable, and baked beans is more common in the winter, while fresh fruits such as melon, watermelons, and cucumbers with cheese and bread or plain yogurt might be served as dinner during the summertime.

Most friend and family gatherings that happen during the weekdays take place at around dinner time. When dinner is prepared for guests, it is no longer just a light meal and normally consists of two or three main dishes such as rice, stew, and meat, as well as several side dishes. Iranian gatherings and parties are famous for سفره رنگین [sofre-ye rangin], colorful food on the dining table or sofre, which is a fabric that is used to cover the carpet when food is served on the floor instead of a dining table.

Short Conversations گفتگوهای کوتاه

In class. listen to the audio files, repeat what you hear and try to fill in the blanks and transcribe the sentences. At home repeat what you hear several times and try to follow the rhythm. Write at least two sentences in Persian about each conversation you hear. During the next class time, you will work with a classmate to create a scenario that uses these expressions.

. چای میل دارید .... قهوه؟

. قهوه می‌خورم. خیلی ....

. چای میل ....؟

. بله، می‌خورم. متشکرم.

c h â y   m e y l ....?

c h â y   m e y l ....?

....

....

.... .۱

.... .۱

.... .۲

.... .۲

. بستنی می‌خوری؟

.... ؟

. نه، مرسی.

....

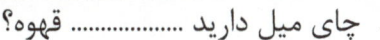

.... .۱

.... .۲

65 PERSIAN OF IRAN TODAY

| ...خوا... | ...ژ... | ...خ...خ... | ...چ... |

Part 1: che /ch/ چ ـچـ ـچ

| قارچ | پیچ | بچّه | چشم |

1. Listen to the audio file for چ che.

The letter *che* is pronounced like the /ch/ in children. It is written exactly like *jim*, but with three dots in a v-shape instead of one.

2. Watch the video and follow the instructions.

چ .... چ ....

3. Watch the video and write the following words.

چیز .... پیچِش .... چِشم ....

بچّه ها .... پارچ .... مُچ ....

4. Listen and check when you hear /ch/ sound in the word.

۱. ☐   ۲. ☐   ۳. ☐   ۴. ☐   ۵. ☐

5. Circle the letters چ in the following texts. Report to your instructor how many چ you identified in the text.

در لحظه‌ای که رشته‌ی آبی رگ‌هایش
مانند مارهای مرده از دو سوی گلوگاهش
بالا خزیده‌اند. (همان، ص۲۳)
این متن- ایمان بیاوریم - با تاثر و حسرت به استغنای معنایی می‌رسد:
چه مهربان بودی ای یار ای یگانه‌ترین یار
چه مهربان بودی وقتی دروغ می‌گفتی
چه مهربان بودی وقتی که پلک‌های آینه را می‌بستی
و چلچراغ‌ها را

6. Listen and write the words you hear.

۱.   ۲.   ۳.   ۴.   ۵.

۶.   ۷.   ۸.   ۹.   ۱۰.

Part 2: khe /kh/ _خ_خـ_ــخــ

| خبر | سخت | میخ | شاخ |

1. Listen to the audio file for خ *khe*.

The sound of the letter *khe* is found in many European languages: the Scottish pronunciation of "loch," and the German "ch" as in "Bach." To pronounce خ , say "k" and pay attention to where the back of your tongue hits the back of the roof of your mouth and blocks your windpipe. Instead of closing off the windpipe with the back of your tongue completely, block it part way, and you will produce this sound. It is written exactly like *jim* and *che*, but with one dot above it.

2. Watch the video and follow the instructions.

خ.......خ.................................

3. Watch the video and write the following words.

خانُم...................دُختَر...................خَبَر...................

بِبَخشید...................اَخبار...................اِختیار...................

نَخ...................شوخ...................سیخ...................

4. Listen and check when you hear the /kh/ sound in the word.

☐ ۱.   ☐ ۲.   ☐ ۳.   ☐ ۴.   ☐ ۵.

---

67 PERSIAN OF IRAN TODAY

5. Circle the letter خ in the following text. Report to your instructor how many خ you identified in the text.

6. Listen and write the words you hear.

۱. ۲. ۳. ۴. ۵.

۶. ۷. ۸. ۹. ۱۰.

Part 3: zhe /zh/ ‎ژ‎

اژدها	مژده	ژاله

1. Listen to the audio file for ژ zhe

This consonant corresponds to a sound for which there is no alphabetic equivalent in English, but the sound does exist in many English words. Its sound is like the "s" in the words "vision" and "treasure."
The letter ژ is a nonconnector and has the same shape as ر and ز, except that it takes three dots above.

2. Watch the video and follow the instructions.

ژ ....

3. Watch the video and write the following words.

ژاپُن .... پَژمُرده .... سوژه ....

4. Listen and write the words you hear.

۱. ۲. ۳. ۴. ۵.

۶. ۷. ۸. ۹. ۱۰.

5. Circle the letters ژ in the following text. Report to your instructor how many ژ you identified in the text.

آن شب ژاله در اُتاقش نشسته بود و با ماژیک هایش چیز های قشنگی می کشید ـ دو روز پیش دایی پژمان برای ژاله کادو های زیادی آورده بود ـ او تازه از ژاپن برگشته بود ـ ژاله از بین کادو ها از ماژیک های پفی بیشتر خوشش می آمد ـ آن شب ژاله آن قدر چیز های قشنگ کشید که ماژیک هایش تمام شد ـ نیمه های شب با شنیدن زمزمه هایی چشمانش را باز کرد ـ کنار دیوار مادربزرگش را دید که ژاکت می بافت ـ سرش را برگرداند و در گوشه ی اُتاقش یک ماشین پژو دید ـ در همین هنگام آمبولانسی که آژیر می کشید ـ از کنارش رد شد ـ

Part 4: khâ /kh/ ___خوا___ | خواب | خواهر |

1. Listen to the audio file for file خوا khâ.

This combination of letters is seen in many common words in Persian. Although a و is written, it remains silent in standard Persian pronunciation. So the combination خوا is pronounced as خا. Look at the following words that contain خوا and try to pronounce them.

2. List of words with خوا :

۱. خواهر   sister
۲. خواستن   to want
۳. خوابیدن to sleep
۴. خوار   small
۵. خواندن   to read

PERSIAN OF IRAN TODAY

3. Connect the letters to form words.

۱. س + ا + ن + دِ + و + ی + چ   ....

۲. مُ + ژ + گ + ا + ن   ....

۳. بَ + خ + ت   ....

۴. مَ + ن + و + چِ + ه + ر   ....

۵. خ + ا + و + ی + ا + ر   ....

۶. خُ + ر + ا + س + ا + ن   ....

4. Listen to the following words. Fill in the missing letter(s) for each word, and then write the complete word on a separate piece of paper.

۱. ــین ....   ۲. رــیم ....   ۳. خــویار ....

۴. شوفا ــ ....   ۵. ــوب ....   ۶. تیراــ ....

۷. ــانویه ....   ۸. باندــژ ....   ۹. خــاسان ....

۱۰. ــاکت ....   ۱۱. چــی ....   ۱۲. ــوش ....

۱۳. چــو ....   ۱۴. اســخراج ....

5. Read the following words aloud with your partner.

۱. پاتیناژ   ۲. خِرَدمَند   ۳. ژانر   ۴. خَبَر   ۵. ژانویه   ۶. واژه

۷. ژن   ۸. مُختار   ۹. پاساژ   ۱۰. اِجرا   ۱۱. ژاپُن   ۱۲. ژاله

۱۳. هُجوم   ۱۴. اِنرژی   ۱۵. پِروژه   ۱۶. مَجارِستان   ۱۷. ژامبون   ۱۸. هِجرَت

۱۹. بیچاره   ۲۰. تِجارَت

6. Listen to the audio file and mark the word you hear.

همان / هِرَم	۷	شاخ / شاه	۱
شهد / شهید	۸	خار / هار	۲
رها / راه	۹	سخی / سهی	۳
سهل / ساحل	۱۰	خر / هر	۴
مرارت / ملالت	۱۱	ماهر / مهر	۵
لام / رام	۱۲	هان / خان	۶

واژگان Vocabulary

1. Listen to and learn these words. Translate the sentences. The spoken variations have been included in parentheses.

sister/ my sister	او خواهرم است. (اون خواهرمه.)	۱. خواهَر/خواهرم
they	آنها سوپ دوست دارند. (اونا سوپ دارن.)	۲. آنها (اونا)
they are	ایرانی هستند. (ایرانی هستن.)	۳. هَستَند
you are	تو دانشجو هستی؟	۴. هَستی
do you eat/drink?	شما شیرینی می‌خورید؟ (شما شیرینی می خورین؟)	۵. می‌خُورید؟ (می‌خورین)
would you like (to have)?	بستنی میل دارید؟ (بستنی میل دارین؟) Used only when offering food or drink. We never use this verb for first person.	۶. مِیل دارید؟ (میل دارین)
I eat, I drink	من شیرینی و بستنی می‌خورم.	۷. می‌خُورم
tea	من چای ایرانی دوست دارم.	۸. چای
cheese	شما پنیر دارید؟ (شما پنیر دارین؟)	۹. پَنیر

English	Example (formal / colloquial)	#	Word
soda	نوشابه میل دارید؟ (نوشابه میل دارین؟)	۱۰-	نوشابه
water	آب می‌خورید؟ (آب می‌خورین؟)	۱۱-	آب
fruit	میوه می‌خورید؟ (میوه می‌خورین؟)	۱۲-	میوه
fruit juice	آب‌میوه میل دارید؟ (آب میوه میل دارین؟)	۱۳-	آب‌میوه
you	تو خواهر داری؟	۱۴-	تو
bad	بد نیستم.	۱۵-	بَد
good	بستنی اینجا خوب است. (بستنی اینجا خوبه)	۱۶-	خوب
street	این خیابان یک رستوران ایرانی دارد. (این خیابون یه رستوران ایرانی داره.)	۱۷-	خیابان
house	این خانه‌ی شماست؟ (این خونه‌ی شماست؟)	۱۸-	خانه (خونه)
in	در تهران هستم. (تهران هستم.)	۱۹-	در (تو)
room	این اتاقِ من است. (این اتاق منه.)	۲۰-	اتاق
window	اتاقِ من پنجره ندارد. (اتاق من نداره.)	۲۱-	پَنجِره/ پنجَره
door	این درِ کلاس است. (این در کلاسه.)	۲۲-	دَر
or	چای میل دارید یا قهوه؟ (چای میل دارین یا قهوه؟)	۲۳-	یا
thank you	خیلی ممنون پدر!	۲۴-	خیلی مَمنون
welcome!	(خیلی خوش اومدین!)	۲۵-	خیلی خوش آمدید!
yes	ایرانی هستید؟ -بله (ایرانی هستین؟)	۲۶-	بله
no	خواهر دارید؟ -نه، ندارم. (خواهر دارین؟-نه، ندارم.)	۲۷-	نه
what	چی میل دارید؟ (چی میل دارین؟)	۲۸-	چه (چی)
dinner	شام سوپ می‌خورم.	۲۹-	شام
lunch	ناهار چی میل دارید؟ (ناهار چی میل دارین؟)	۳۰-	ناهار/ نهار

2. Listen to the audio file again. Based on what you hear, write the vowel on the example sentences. Now listen to the next audio file. Write the sentences you hear and translate them to English.

Listening Comprehension   درک شنیدار

1. Watch the videos and answer the following questions in Persian.

   1. What does Shayli eat for breakfast?
   2. Does she drink coffee?
   3. Listen carefully and guess what "delicious" is in Persian?
   4. How does she say "Yummy!" in Persian?

2. Watch the video and write what you hear.

PERSIAN OF IRAN TODAY

Grammar Note / یادداشت دستوری

Possession

In Persian, possessive adjectives (his, her, my, etc.) are expressed in two different ways, both of which you've heard before.

1. The first way is to use the personal pronouns that you already know. For example, think of how you learned to ask someone his or her name.

اسم شما چیه؟

Which part of that sentence is "your name"?

………………………………………………………………………………………………

You will notice that when we form possessive structures in this way, we put the thing being possessed (اسم) first and the pronoun (شما) second. We don't write anything in between these two words, but what do we say in between them?

………………………………………………………………………………………………

So to review, when you want to create possession using the personal pronouns, you put the main noun first connect it to the pronoun with an /e/ sound.

Try filling out the chart below to learn how to ask other people's names as well.

	ما		من
اسمِ شما	شما		تو
	آنها		او

2. The second form uses suffixes that are attached directly to the thing being possessed. Consider the following example from your most recent vocabulary list. What changes do you see?

………………………………………………………………………………………………

sister	خواهر
my sister	خواهرَم

Every pronoun in Persian has a suffix equivalent. Don't confuse these possessive endings with the verbal endings that you've learned (even though the first-person singular is the same). Fill in the chart below, using the information you know to extract new information.

من	خواهرَم	my sister	ـَم
تو	خواهرَت (خواهرِت)	your sister	
او (اون)	خواهرَش (خواهرِش)	his / her sister	
شما	خواهرِتان (خواهرِتون)	your sister	
ما	خواهرِمان (خواهرِمون)	our sister	
آن‌ها (اونا)/ ایشان (ایشون)	خواهرِشان (خواهرِشون)	his/their sister	

Combine the following nouns and pronouns to create a possessive structure.

۱	خواهر	+	ما	=	خواهر ما	خواهرمان (خواهرمون)
۲	برادر	+	تو	=	....	....
۳	پدر	+	آنها	=	....	....
۴	دوست	+	او	=	....	....
۵	پنیر	+	من	=	....	....
۶	مادر	+	شما	=	....	....

A Point of Clarification

Look over the exercise that you just completed. As you can see, we have two ways of expressing possession in Persian. But what's the difference between these two ways? Can you guess?

The difference is very slight, but when you use the full pronoun, you are adding a little more emphasis to that person. Of course, we encourage you to incorporate both ways into your speaking and writing.

###

You remember from the previous unit that a question has the same word order as its statement counterpart. In the written style, however, sometimes the sentence is so long that it is hard to know if it is a question or a statement. You have to go all the way to the end of the sentence to see if there is a question mark at the end, and then go back and read the sentence in raising tone. There is a solution for this problem. Many writers use a particle in the beginning of a yes/no question (a yes/no question is a question which has a potential yes or no as its answer, like the sentences which start with do, does, and did in English). This particle is "آیا".

Read the following examples:

آیا شما در این خیابان زندگی می‌کنید؟
آیا دوستان پدرتان بستنی و شیرینی دوست دارند؟
آیا دوستان‌تان ژاپنی هستند؟

Write 3 questions starting with آیا.

۱...

۲...

۳...

Grammar Exercises

1. Complete the chart below for the verb "to eat" in the present tense.

می‌خوریم	ما	می‌خورم	مَن
.... (............)	شُما	.... (............)	شما/تو
می‌خورند	آنها/ ایشان (اونا)	می‌خورند	ایشان/او (ایشون/اون)

2. Match the following vocabulary words to their corresponding picture and write a sentence for each word.

پنیر   چای   خواهرم   نان

3. Fill in the blanks and then answer the questions. Use written form to answer the questions.

۱. چای می‌خورید؟ (چای می‌خورین) ....

۲. برادرتان نان می‌خورد؟ (برادرتون .... می‌خوره؟) ....

۳. خواهرتان پنیر می‌خورد؟ (خواهرتون ....؟) ....

۴. نان نمی‌خوریم؟ (......... نمی‌خوریم؟) ....

۵. این سخت است؟ (این ....؟) ....

۶. خوبی؟ (خوبی؟) ....

نوشتن Writing Exercise

Use the words from the vocabulary you have learned to write a conversation with 10 sentences. Your topic is

چی میل دارید؟

حرف زدن Speaking Activities

Homework:

Review the vocabulary and the grammar (possessive pronouns) of this unit and think about how you would ask your classmates the following questions in **spoken** Persian. Practice them aloud several times so you will be ready to use these questions in class.

~ Do you eat cheese?
~ Does your mother drink tea? (for "drink," use the same verb you would use for "to eat")
~ Is your professor Japanese?
~ Does your father like cheese?
~ Does your brother eat bread?
~ Is that a window?!
~ Does your room have a window?
~ What do you eat for lunch and dinner?

In Class:

Ask your classmates the questions that you translated for homework. Be sure to say "Thank you!" to everyone you speak with and "You're Welcome!" /khâhesh mikonam/ to anyone who thanks you. Pay attention to what your classmates say, because your instrutor may ask you to report what you've learned!

Classroom Activities

فعالیت‌های پیشنهادی برای کلاس

1. **Odd Man Out**: Work with one partner and have a short conversation in Persian. Find out as much information about your partner as you can using the vocabulary that you know (focus especially on the vocabulary from Unit 4. Then, with your partner write three questions that use the new vocabulary and contain the possessive pronouns that you learned in this lesson.

Now, work with another group and use the questions you wrote to ask one person in the other group about his/her partner.

2. **Your New Best Friend**: Your instructor will give you a card with information about your new best friend. Work with your partner who will try to get as much information about your new friend as possible. After 10 minutes you will introduce your partner's friend to the class.

درس پنجم
UNIT 5

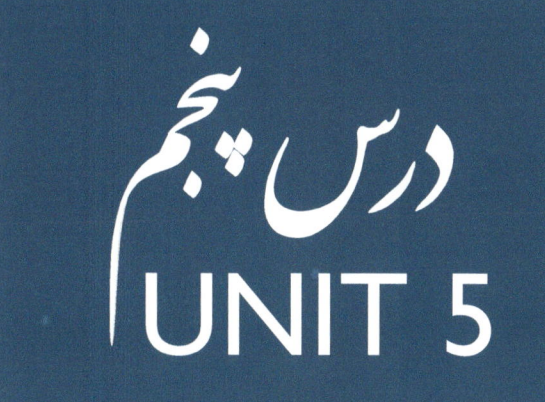

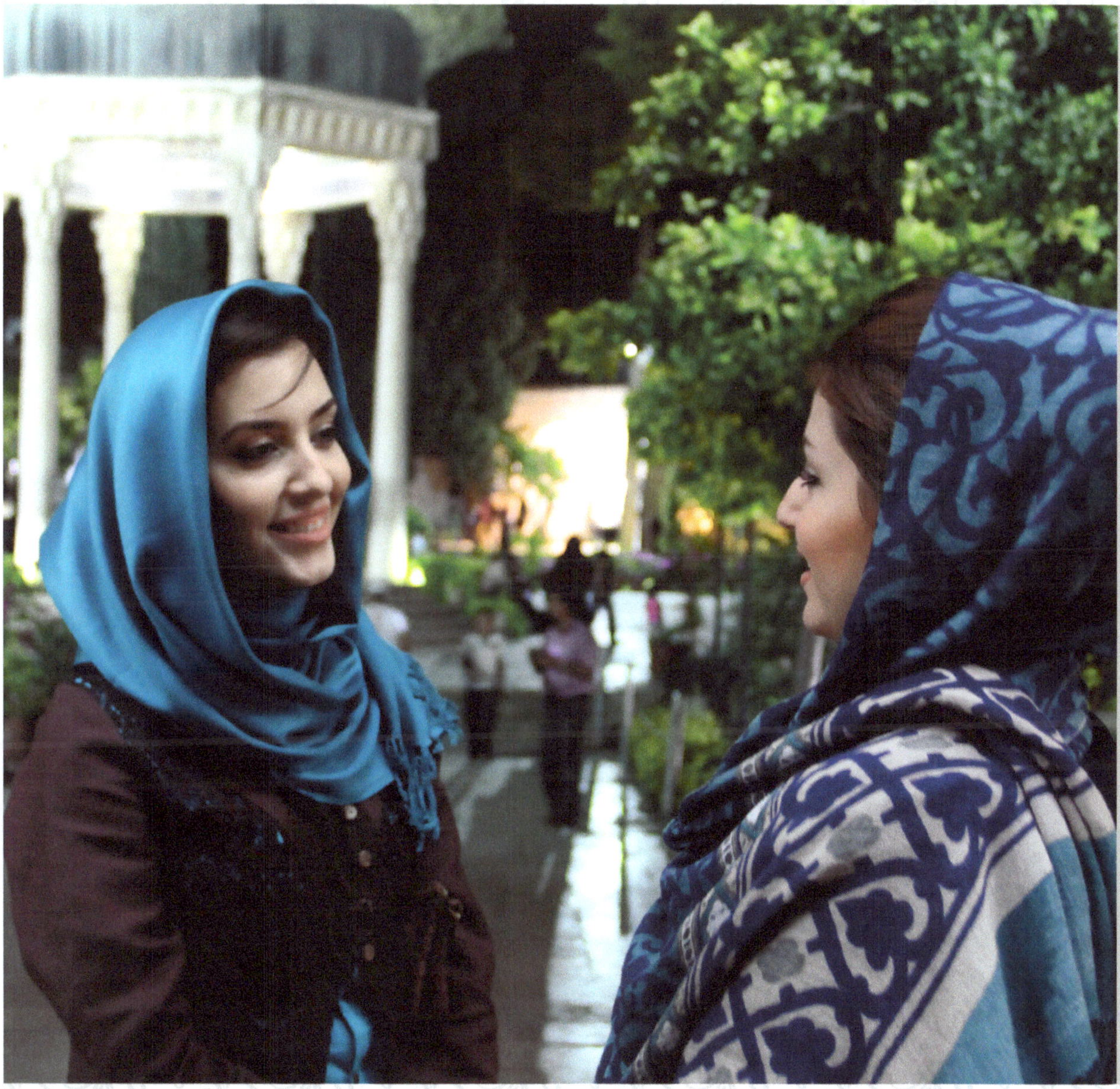

ص	آ
ض	ب
ط	پ
ظ	ت
ع	ث
غ	ج
ف	چ
ق	ح
ک	خ
گ	د
ل	ذ
م	ر
ن	ز
و	ژ
ه	س
ی	ش

Where are you from? شما کجایی هستید؟ / اهل کجایید؟

Cultural Note یادداشت فرهنگی

Diverse Iran

While Persian is the national language of Iran, only about 51% of Iranians speak Persian as their native language. Historically, Persian has always been a major literary language in Iran and the greater Persianate world, but it emerged as the unifying language in Iran with the rise of nationalism during the late nineteenth and early twentieth centuries. Since then, almost all official means of communication has been and is conducted in Persian, which is true for major media outlets, schools, and government correspondences. Despite this, Iran is home to several ethno-linguistic minorities, including Turks, Kurds, Armenians, and Arabs, all whom have their own cultural practices and languages. Iran's diversity was even acknowledged in its first national anthem, which concluded with a line about the many languages and colors found among Iranians. Even so, the anthem was written in Persian, signaling the importance of the language in Iranian nationalism.

The diversity of Iran is not limited to ethno-linguistic groups. Because Iran did not have a strong central government until fairly recently in the early twentieth century, strong regional identities developed, and major cities and provinces are identifiable by their accents, handcrafts, and foods. Although some minorities are concentrated in specific regions, such as the Baluch in southeastern Iran, most tend to be scattered across the Iranian plateau. Many Iranians continue to be proud of both their ethnic and regional affiliations.

While the answer to the question اهل کجا هستین؟ is usually one's hometown, some people may continue by introducing their ethnicity. For example, one may answer:

اهل خرم آباد هستم، ما بختیاری هستیم.

Short Conversations گفتگوهای کوتاه

In class listen to the audio files, repeat what you hear and try to fill in the blanks. At home repeat what you hear several times and try to follow the rhythm. Write at least two sentences in Persian about each conversation you hear. During the next class time, you will work with a classmate to create a scenario that uses these expressions.

. سلام. من ....
. سلام، من .... هستم. خیلی خوشوقتم.
. شما .... کجایید؟
. من کرمانی هستم. شما .... هستید؟
. من اهل .... هستم.

1. ....
2. ....

. اسم من شیماست. .... ؟
. اسم من زهراست.
. اهل .... هستین؟
. نه، ....

1. ....
2. ....

. شما اهل .... هستید؟
. نه، .... شما .... هستید؟
. من .... هستم.

1. ....
2. ....

...گ..گ...	...ک..ک...	...ق..ق...	...ف..ف...

Part 1: fe /f/ ___ف___ ف

فردا	مفید	کیف	برف

1. Listen to the audio file for ف fe.

This letter is pronounced like the English "f" as in "feather." ف is a connecting letter with a relatively stable shape. Its independent and final forms have a tail that remains on the line.

2. Watch the video and follow the instructions.

ف........ف..

3. Watch the video and write the following words.

فَرش................... سَفَر................... آفتاب...................

سِفید................... لیف................... رَفتَم...................

4. Listen and check when you hear the /f/ sound in the word.

☐ ۱.   ☐ ۲.   ☐ ۳.   ☐ ۴.   ☐ ۵.

5. Circle the letter ف in the following text. Report to your instructor how many ف you identified in the text.

من همیشه از مفهوم سمبول نفرت داشته‌ام و از تکرار این قضیه خسته نمی‌شوم که من در زمان تدریس، شاگردی را رفوزه کردم به این سبب که در ورقه امتحان گفته بود جین آستین برگها را وصف می‌کند و آنها را «سبز» می‌خواند چرا که فانی دلی پر از امید دارد و سبز علامت امیدواری است. ناباکوف این گونه تفسیر را پوشلوست می‌نامد.

6. Listen and write the words you hear.

۱.   ۲.   ۳.   ۴.   ۵.

۶.   ۷.   ۸.   ۹.   ۱۰.

Part 2: qâf /q/   ــــقـــــق | قرمز | مقبره | قاشق | برق |

1. Listen to the audio file for ق qâf.

This letter represents a sound with no equivalent in English. Its sound is somewhat like a mix between a deep /g/ mixed with *khe*. It is pronounced far back in the throat, at the very back of the tongue.

Take a minute to become more familiar with your throat muscles. Open your mouth and say aah, as if you were at the doctor. Your tongue should be flat in your mouth. Without raising your tongue, pull it back so that the base of your tongue closes off air by pulling back against the throat. At this point, you should not be able to breathe through your mouth, although it is wide open. Practice doing this first without making a sound. After performing this exercise several times, make a sound by releasing the air forcefully and allowing your vocal cords to vibrate. The result will be the sound ق. Listen to the examples to hear how ق is pronounced.

2. Watch the video and follow the instructions.

ق............ق

3. Watch the video and write the following words.

قالی .... دَقیقه .... آقا ....

اِنقِلاب .... قاشُق .... اُتاق ....

بوق .... قِرمِز .... مَقاله ....

4. Listen and check when you hear the /q/ sound in the word.

١.   ٢.   ٣.   ٤.   ٥.

٦.   ٧.   ٨.   ٩.   ١٠.

5. Circle the letters ف in the following texts. Report to your instructor how many ف you identified in the text.

6. Listen and write the words you hear.

١.   ٢.   ٣.   ٤.   ٥.

٦.   ٧.   ٨.   ٩.   ١٠.

| کنار | مکان | اشک | پاک |

Part 3: *kâf* /k/   __ک__ــکــ ک

1. Listen to the audio file for ک *kâf*.

This letter corresponds to English *k* as in *likewise*. However, the way it is pronounced is slightly different.

2. Watch the video and follow the instructions.

ک . . . ک . . .

3. Watch the video and write the following words.

کار .... کَمَر .... کِتاب ....
اِستِکان .... شِکَر .... فِکر ....
بانک .... تیک تاک .... پَشمَک ....

4. Listen and check when you hear the /k/ sound in the word.

☐ ۱.   ☐ ۲.   ☐ ۳.   ☐ ۴.   ☐ ۵.   ☐ ۶.   ☐ ۷.   ☐ ۸.

5. Circle the letter ک in the following text. Report to your instructor how many ک you identified in the text.

زبان بدن در فرهنگ‌ها و کشورهای دیگر، معنی مشترک و یکسانی دارد. معروف است که می‌گویند همه به یک زبان سکوت می‌کنند. اما برخی از نشانه‌های زبان بدن در هر کشوری، معنی خودش را دارد. مثلاً علامت شست دست در کشورهای انگلیسی زبان به معنای OK است. در بعضی کشورها اگر شست خیلی بالا بیاید معنای خوبی ندارد.

در آمریکا اگر بخواهند مجانی سوار ماشین شوند، کنار جاده می‌ایستند و شست خود را در امتداد جاده حرکت می‌دهند. اگر همین حرکت را در کشوری آسیایی انجام دهید، شاید کار به مشاجره بکشد. شاید هم راننده‌ای متعصب و غیور شما را با ماشینش زیر بگیرد.

6. Listen and write the words you hear.

۱.   ۲.   ۳.   ۴.   ۵.

۶.   ۷.   ۸.   ۹.   ۱۰.

85   PERSIAN OF IRAN TODAY

Part 4: gâf /g/ ‗گ‗گ‗ گ | گرم | مگر | سنگ | برگ |

1. Listen to the audio file for گ gâf.

This letter corresponds to English "g" as in "goal." It is written exactly like kaaf, but with a short line drawn above it following the contour of the letter.

2. Watch the video and follow the instructions.

گ .... گ ....

3. Watch the video and write the following words.

گوش .... گَشتَن .... مَگَر ....

نهنگ .... جَنگ .... مَرگ ....

4. Listen and check when you hear the /g/ sound in the word.

۱. ☐   ۲. ☐   ۳. ☐   ۴. ☐   ۵. ☐

۶. ☐   ۷. ☐   ۸. ☐   ۹. ☐   ۱۰. ☐

5. Circle the letter گ in the following text. Report to your instructor how many گ you identified in the text.

گشت جهان همچو نگار ای غلام   بادۀ گلرنگ بیار ای غلام
با گل و با بلبل و با مل بهم   وصل طلب فصل بهار ای غلام
بلبل عاشق به صبوحی دَرست   می‌شنوی نالۀ زار ای غلام
نرگس سرمست نگر کاو فکند   سر ز گرانی به کنار ای غلام
پیش نشین تازه بکن کار آب   بیش مبر آب ز کار ای غلام
آب بده زانکه جهان هر نفس   خاک کند چون تو هزار ای غلام
زخم خمارم چو به زاری بکشت   نوش خمارم ز خُم آر ای غلام

6. Listen and write the words you hear.

۱.   ۲.   ۳.   ۴.   ۵.

۶.   ۷.   ۸.   ۹.   ۱۰.

۱۱.   ۱۲.   ۱۳.   ۱۴.   ۱۵.

7. Connect the letters to form words.

۱. فِ + م + ی + ن + ی + س + م   ....

۲. م + و + س + ی + ق + ی   ....

۳. ل + ی + ف   ....

۴. شَ + فَ + ق   ....

۵. آ + ف + ر + ی + ق + ا   ....

۶. تِ + ر + ا + ف + ی + ک   ....

۷. و + ا + شَ + ن + گ + تُ + ن   ....

8. You will hear some words. For each, write the missing letter(s) in the blank and rewrite the word on a separate piece of paper.

۱. فر‍‍ـشنده   ۲. شیکا‍ـو   ۳. رادیـــال   ۴. یو‍ـا

۵. پُرو‍ـُسور   ۶. قا‍ـله   ۷. تونـ‍   ۸. آمریـــا

۹. کار‍ـر   ۱۰. مالـ‍   ۱۱. ‍ـرانسه   ۱۲. ‍ـلستان

۱۳. کنـ‍ـرانس   ۱۴. افـ‍ـار   ۱۵. ‍ـانون   ۱۶. ‍ـابینه

۱۷. ر‍ـابت   ۱۸. ‍ـودتا   ۱۹. ‍ـوری   ۲۰. کِـ‍

۲۱. تانـ‍ـو   ۲۲. اشتـ‍ـاق

9. Read aloud the following word with your partner.

١. سَفَر ٢. اِسکی ٣. فوتبال
٤. کُنسول ٥. فَلسَفه ٦. کُمیته
٧. قِرقیزِستان ٨. کانادا ٩. قَزاقِستان
١٠. کِراوات ١١. اُفُق ١٢. رُمانتیک
١٣. قوری ١٤. کامیون ١٥. تَقدیم
١٦. گَرم ١٧. سَنگ ١٨. گُرسنه
١٩. جمهوری چِک ٢٠. بُزُرگ

10. Listen to the audio file and mark the word you hear.

سوق / سوگ	١	قوری / گوری	٧
گرم / قرن	٢	مگر / مقر	٨
نقاد / نگار	٣	اگر / اقل	٩
قریب / گلیم	٤	گوش / قوچ	١٠
قراین / گلایه	٥	شقاوت / شکایت	١١
گاری / قاری	٦	مشق / مشک	١٢

11. In Class: Read the texts and guess what they are. What are some words that you know? (source: Vaseteh.com)

فروش
کامپیوتر نوت بوک، DELL، نو

توضیحات:

TESHSA-ALL BRANDS OF LAPTOP
Tehran Office:
Dubai Office: +۹۷۱۵۰۷۸۴۹۰۱۴   +۹۸۲۱-۵۵۸۰۷۳۷۲
Canada Office: +۱-۴۱۶۳۰۲۸۰۶۰

معینی
تلفن: ۵۵۸۰۷۳۷۲
استان: تهران
شهر: تهران

فروش
قیمت ۸,۸۰۰,۰۰۰ تومان

تویوتا، مدل ۱۹۹۱، ۶ دنده، دفرنسیال عقب، ۴ در، کولردار، پلاک لیزری، مجهز به دزدگیر، رنگ سفید، رنگ شده، موتور ۲۰۰۰، ۴ سیلندر، اتاق سالم، لاستیک ۹۰٪، موتور سالم، گیربکس، دیفرانسیل سالم، داشبورد سالم، تودوزی سالم

نیمه فول، فرمان هیدرولیک، گرمکن شیشه عقب، معاینه فنی
لوازم اضافی:
روکش صندلی، رادیو پخش، کنسول وسط
جهان پناه:
تلفن: ۰۹۳۵۳۷۶۱۰۷۰
موبایل: ۰۹۱۲۴۲۳۱۰۰۲
تعداد دفعات بازدید: ۱۶۹۸۳ مرتبه

Vocabulary 1 واژگان ۱

1. Listen to and learn these words. Translate the sentences. The spoken variations have been included in parentheses.

English	Example	Persian
thank you	متشکّرم مادر.	۱. متشکّرم
you're welcome	خواهش می‌کُنَم.	۲. خواهِش می‌کُنَم
excuse me	ببخشید، شما دانشجو هستید؟ (ببخشید، شما دانشجو هستین؟)	۳. ببخشید
class	کلاس فارسی دارم.	۴. کِلاس
university	ما در دانشگاه هستیم. (ما تو/توی دانشگاه هستیم.)	۵. دانشگاه
sir, gentleman, man	آقا، شما ایرانی هستید؟ (آقا، شما ایرانی هستین؟)	۶. آقا
ma'am, lady, Mrs., Miss	این خانم دانشجو است. (...دانشجوه.)	۷. خانُم
Persian	ایشان استاد فارسی هستند. (ایشون استاد فارسی هستن.)	۸. فارسی
I know (how to do something), you know	تو فارسی بلدی؟	۹. بَلَدَم، بَلَدی
I know (knowledge)	نمی‌دانم کلاس داریم یا نه. / فارسی می‌دانم	۱۰. می‌دانم (می‌دونم)
you know	اسم او را می‌دانی؟ (اسم اونو می‌دونی؟)	۱۱. می‌دانی (می‌دونی)
English	من انگلیسی بلد نیستم.	۱۲. انگلیسی
I live	من در تهران زندگی می‌کنم. (من تو تهران زندگی می‌کنم.)	۱۳. زندگی می‌کنم
with	من با پدر و مادرم زندگی می‌کنم.	۱۴. با
coffee	ببخشید، قهوه دارید؟ (ببخشید، قهوه دارین؟)	۱۵. قَهوه
United States	این جا آمریکا است. (این جا آمریکاست.)	۱۶. آمریکا
American	آنها آمریکایی هستند. (اونا آمریکایی هستن.)	۱۷. آمریکایی
soccer	من فوتبال دوست دارم.	۱۸. فوتبال
street	خانه‌ی ما در خیابان کاج است. (خونه‌ی ما تو خیابون کاجه.)	۱۹. خیابان (خیابون)
here	کلاس تو اینجاست؟	۲۰. اینجا/ این جا
there	خواهرم آنجا است. (خواهرم اونجاست.)	۲۱. آنجا (اونجا)
where-where is it?	کلاس فارسی کجاست؟	۲۲. کجا، کجاست
how many	این کلاس چند دانشجو دارد؟ (...چند تا دانشجو داره؟)	۲۳. چند (چند تا)
how old are you?	(شما چند سالتونه؟)	۲۴. (چند سالتونه؟) = چند سال دارید؟
I am twenty.	(بیست و چهار سالمه.)	۲۵. (بیست سالمه.) = بیست سال دارم.
He is twenty years old.	(اون پسر بیست سالشه.)	۲۶. (بیست سالشه.) = بیست سال دارد.

2. Listen to the audio file again. Based on what you hear, write the vowels on the example sentences. Now listen to the next audio file. Write the sentences you hear and translate them to English.

واژگان ۲   Vocabulary 2

3. Listen to and learn these words. Translate the sentences. The spoken variations have been included in parentheses.

one	یک برادر دارم. (یه برادر دارم.)	یِک	۱.
two	دو برادر دارد. (دو تا برادر داره.)	دو	۲.۲
three	سه برادر دارند. (سه تا برادر دارن.)	سه	۳.
four	چهار برادر دارید؟ (چاهار تا برادر دارین؟)	چُهار (چاهار)	۴.
five	پنج خواهر هستیم. (پنج تا خواهر هستیم.)	پَنج	۵.
six	شش برادر هستند. (شیش تا برادر هستن.)	شِش (شیش)	۶.
seven	هفت دوست ایرانی دارم. (هفت تا دوست ایرانی دارم.)	هَفت	۷.
eight	هشت دوست آمریکایی داری؟ (هشت تادوست آمریکایی داری؟)	هَشت	۸.
nine	نه دانشجو در کلاس هستند. (نه تا دانشجو تو کلاس هستن.)	نُه	۹.
ten	ده آمریکایی آنجا هستند. (ده تا آمریکایی اونجا هستن.)	دَه	۱۰.
eleven	یازده ژاپنی اینجا هستند. (یازده تا ژاپنی اینجا هستن.)	یازدَه	۱۱.
twelve	دوازده دانشجوی ایرانی در دانشگاه هستند. (دوازده تا دانشجوی ایرانی تو دانشگاه هستن.)	دَوازدَه	۱۲.
thirteen	اینجا سیزده دانشگاه داریم. (اینجا سیزده تا دانشگاه داریم.)	سیزدَه	۱۳.
fourteen	چهارده نان دارم. (چاهارده تا نون دارم.)	چُهاردَه (چاردَه)	۱۴.
fifteen	پانزده استاد داریم. (پونزده تا استاد داریم.)	پانزدَه (پونزده)	۱۵.
sixteen	شانزده دانشجو دارد. (شونزده تا دانشجو داره.)	شانزدَه (شونزده)	۱۶.
seventeen	اینجا هفده کلاس داریم. (اینجا هیوده تا کلاس داریم.)	هفدَه (هیوده)	۱۷.
eighteen	هجده خانم در کلاس هستند. (هیژده تا خانم توی کلاس هستن.)	هِجدَه (هیژده)	۱۸.
nineteen	نوزده آقا در کلاس هستند. (نوزده آقا توی کلاس هستن.)	نوزدَه	۱۹.
twenty / thirty	این دانشگاه بیست استاد آمریکایی دارد. (این دانشگاه بیست تا استاد آمریکایی داره.)	بیست، سی	۲۰.

4. Listen to the audio file again. Based on what you hear, write the vowels on the example sentences. Now listen to the next audio file. Write the sentences you hear and translate them to English.

In class:

1. Listen to your instructor ask questions like "how many students are there in the class?" and answer the questions.

2. Your instructor will ask you to do some addition. Listen carefully and answer the questions.

Vocabulary 3   واژگان ۳

5. Vocabulary you already know! Listen to and learn these words. Translate the sentences.

English	Persian Sentence	Persian Word
park	یک پارک در این خیابان است. (یک پارک توی این خیابونه.)	۱. پارک
villa	ما یک ویلا در تهران داریم. (ما یه ویلا تو تهران داریم.)	۲. ویلا
doctor	او دکتر شماست؟ (اون دکتر شماست؟)	۳. دکتر
concert	من کنسرت راک دوست دارم.	۴. کنسرت
movie theater	پنج سینما در این خیابان است. (پنج تا سینما تو این خیابونه.)	۵. سینما
super market	پدرم سوپر مارکت دارد. (پدرم سوپر مارکت داره.)	۶. سوپر مارکت
ski	اسکی دوست ندارم.	۷. اسکی
tennis	خواهرم تنیس دوست دارد. (خواهرم تنیس دوست داره.)	۸. تنیس
opera	اپرا دوست داری؟	۹. اپرا
radio	رادیو کجاست؟	۱۰. رادیو
jacket	ژاکت پدرم این جا است. (ژاکت پدرم این جاست.)	۱۱. ژاکت
marker	ماژیک داری؟	۱۲. ماژیک
television	دو تلویزیون در این اتاق است. (دو تا تلویزیون توی این اتاقه.)	۱۳. تلویزیون

6. Listen to the audio file again. Based on what you hear, write the vowels on the example sentences. Now listen to the next audio file. Write the sentences you hear and translate them to English.

PERSIAN OF IRAN TODAY

7. Look at the following list of countries and the corresponding nationalities. Read them aloud with your partner, and try to discover the rule for forming nationalities from country names. Do they all follow the rule? Circle the ones that don't follow the rule.

 7

مِلّیَّت	کِشوَر
تاجیک	تاجیکستان
کانادایی	کانادا
ژاپنی	ژاپن
اسپانیایی	اسپانیا
انگلیسی	انگلیس
چینی	چین
سوری	سوریه
مکزیکی	مکزیک
پاکستانی	پاکستان
روس	روسیه
اهل ارمنستان	ارمنستان
اهل ترکیه	ترکیه
اهل قزاقستان	قزاقستان
کره‌ای	کره

 8

اهل	شهر
اهل نیویورک	نیویورک
اهل دالاس	دالاس
اهل لس آنجلس	لس آنجلس
اهل واشنگتن	واشنگتن
اهل استانبول	استانبول
اهل دوشنبه	دوشنبه
اهل اسلام آباد	اسلام آباد
اهل لندن	لندن
کابلی / اهل کابل	کابل
شیرازی/ اهل شیراز	شیراز
مشهدی/ اهل مشهد	مشهد

Spelling Note

When we add ی to a word, it may pronunced ye or i, depending on the role of ی. If it's pronunced /i/, the following rule will be applied in writing the word.

/…vowels*/ + /i/ *except for e	/…â/ + /i/ /…u/ + /i/ /…o/ + /i/	آمریکا + ی: آمریکایی کَمرو + ی: کَمرویی نو + ی: نویی
/…consonant/ + /i/	/…b, p, t, d, s, j, etc/ + /i/	مشهد + ی: مشهدی شیراز + ی: شیرازی چین + ی: چینی
/…e/ + /i/	/…e/ + /i/	ترکیه + ی: ترکیه‌ای

Note that the sound /i:/ is different from /y/. For example:

u âmrikâ-i ast	او آمریکایی است.
âmrikâ-ye jonubi	آمریکای جنوبی

Listening Comprehension درک شنیدار

1. Watch the videos and answer the following questions in written Persian.

1. How many languages does Shayli know? What are they?
2. What time does Shayli have class today? What is the class?
3. When does she go to دانشگاه ?
4. How many minutes (دقیقه) is it from Lake Austin Street to school by bus?
5. How many Iranian friends does Shayli have in Austin? How many American friends?
6. What do two American friends of Shayli like?
7. What time is Shayli planning to go to her friend's house today?
8. Does Shayli like football?

2. Watch the videos and write what you hear in Persian.

۱. ....؟

.... ، همین جاست.

۲. ....؟

....

۳. ....؟

....

3. Listen to the audio files and fill in the blanks.

A

من .... هستم. .... سال
دارم. .... و .... دوست دارم.
.... دوم دانشگاه هستم. ....
هستم. .... و .... و
.... می‌دونم.

B

من شایان هستم و .... سالمه.
.... دوست دارم. سال ....
دانشگاه و اهل .... و
.... بلدم.

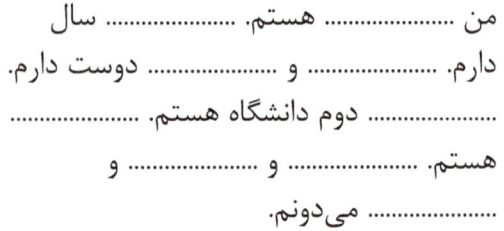

C

- سلام.
- اسمتون چیه؟
- ....
- شما .... ؟
- ....
- .... تلفنتون چنده؟
- ۹۷۶-۲۳۴۵-۴۳۵۶

D

- سلام من .... هستم.
- سلام .... هستم. شما اهل کجا .... ؟
- اهل .... هستم.
- دوشنبه کجاست؟
- دوشنبه در .... است.
- شما .... کجایید؟
- من .... هستم.

یادداشت دستوری — Grammar Note

Using Pronouns

In Persian, the use of nominal pronouns such as من or شما with verbs is somewhat redundant. You don't usually need to say the nominal pronoun before conjugated verbs. The conjugated form of the verb, together with the context, will generally make it clear who the subject of the sentence is. Native speakers of Persian will generally drop the pronoun, and we recommend that you do also.

چای نمی‌خورم.

کجا هستید؟

Present Tense Conjugation

The present tense in Persian has much wider use than the present tense in English. In Persian, we can use the present tense to express actions that are occuring right now or habitually or actions in the future. While there is a future tense in Persian, in spoken Persian we almost always use the present tense to indicate future. At this point, you have learned three verbs in the present tense, "to have," "to be," and "to eat" (in your most recent vocabulary list). Think about these three verbs in the present tense. How is "to eat" different from "to be" and "to have"? The present tense of "to eat" starts with the prefix می . Even though you learned "to be" and "to have" first, they are, in fact, the two most common **irregular** verbs in the present tense. As you learn the patterns and rules for the regular present-tense verbs, don't forget that "to be" and "to have" are the exceptions! Verbs must be conjugated for person and number in Persian. This is done by adding prefixes and suffixes to the verb stems. In general, regular verbs in Persian are conjugated in the present tense according to the following pattern:

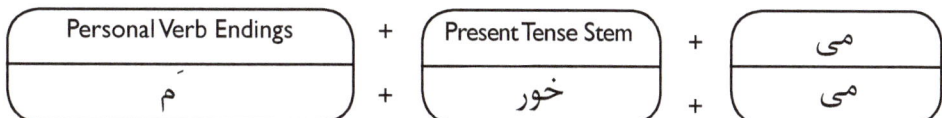

Look at the chart below, which features the present tense conjugations for a verb you know.

Note that می is written in an unconnected form even though ی is generally a connecting letter. This is just a spelling convention.

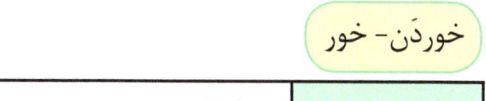

من	می‌خورَم	
تو	می‌خوری	
او (اون)	می‌خورَد (می‌خوره)	
ما	می‌خوریم	
شما	می‌خورید (می‌خورین)	
آنها (اونا)	می‌خورَند (می‌خورن)	

Negating "to eat"

Here are the negative forms for all pronouns. Read carefully and explain the rule. Negating all present-tense verbs except for the verbs "to be" and "to have" follow the same rule. Complete the spoken column with the appropriate words.

Pronoun	Negation of verb "to eat"	Spoken form of Negation forms of "to eat"
من	نِمی‌خورَم	
تو	نِمی‌خوری	
او (اون)	نِمی‌خورَد	
ما	نِمی‌خوریم	
شما	نِمی‌خورید	
آنها (اونا)	نِمی‌خورَند	

Counting

Examine the following example sentences from your vocabulary list (p. 105).

۱. هفت دوست ایرانی دارم.

۲. این دانشگاه بیست استاد آمریکایی دارد.

۳. هجده خانم در کلاس هستند.

What do you notice about the nouns that follow the verbs?

………………………………………………………………………………………

………………………………………………………………………………………

Although you will learn more about counting in Lesson 9, for now keep in mind that in Persian numbers are always followed by singular nouns!

Grammar Exercises

1. Complete with the negative of "to be".

۱. من دانشجو ……………… .

۲. این کلاس ……………… .

۳. شما دانشجو ……………… .

۴. او استاد ……………… .

۵. ما دانشجو ……………… .

2. Fill in the blank with the appropriate words.

می‌خوریم / می‌خورید / هستید / نمی‌خورم

۱. من پپسی ……………… .

۲. آب ………………؟

۳. من و برادرم آب سیب ……………… .

۴. شما اهل کجا ………………

3. Organize the following sets of words into meaningful sentences.

۱. است، کلاس، فارسی، ما، اینجا ……………… .

۲. هستیم، ما، دانشجو ……………… .

۳. من، نیستم، آستین، اهل ……………… .

۴. ندارد، او، کتاب. ……………… .

4. Match the following words to their corresponding picture and write a sentence for each word. In each sentence use a number you have learned in this unit.

    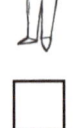     

۱. دانشگاه   ۲. خیابان   ۳. خانم   ۴. اینجا   ۵. آمریکا   ۶. نه   ۷. آقا

Speaking Activities   حرف زدن

In Class:

1. First, complete the spoken column with the appropriate words. Then ask your classmates where their family members live. Report your findings to your instructor.

زندگی کردَن- زندگی کن

Negation of "to live"	Verb "to live" spoken form	Pronoun
....	زندگی می‌کنم	من
....	....	تو
....	....	او (اون)
....	....	ما
....	زندگی می‌کنین	شما
....	....	آنها (اونا)

Your Notes:

2. Do the following exercise step by step.

2–1. Read the questions in the first box and ask three classmates to answer them.

2–2. Your classmates will probably answer your question in the format of the second box. Take notes of what you will learn about your classmates in the boxes and be ready to report the information to the class.

2–3. Report to the class what you have learned. The format of your report should have the format of the third box. Use the format of box number four if you would like to use respectful form.

اسم: .... سن: .... اهل: .... محل زندگی: .... با .... زندگی می‌کند.	(اسم شما چیه*؟ چند سالتونه*؟ کجایی هستید؟ کجا زندگی می‌کنید؟ با پدر و مادرتون زندگی می‌کنید؟) ۱

97 PERSIAN OF IRAN TODAY

اسم: .... سن: .... اهل: .... محل زندگی: .... با .... زندگی می‌کند.	۲ (اسم من سمانه است. نوزده سالمه. کرمانی هستم و با پدر و مادرم در تهران زندگی می‌کنم.)
اسم: .... سن: .... اهل: .... محل زندگی: .... با .... زندگی می‌کند.	۳ (اسم اون سمانه است. نوزده سالشه. کرمانیه و با پدر و مادرش در تهران زندگی می‌کنه.)
اسم: .... سن: .... اهل: .... محل زندگی: .... با .... زندگی می‌کند.	۴ (اسم ایشون سمانه است. نوزده سالشونه. کرمانی هستند و با پدر و مادرشون در تهران زندگی می‌کنن.)

3–1. First, try to figure out what each of these languages is. There may be some letters that you haven't learned yet, but do your best. Once you have figured them all out, your instructor can help you pronounce them.

فارسی، انگلیسی، فرانسه/ فرانسوی، عربی، اسپانیایی، اردو، هندی، ژاپنی، چینی، پرتغالی /porteqâli/ /arabi/

Now, using بلد find out from your classmates what language they speak. Be sure to greet them politely first! Later, you will report to the class what you have learned.

3–2. Practice with خوردن! find out from your classmates what kinds of food (غذا /qazâ/) they like. Some of the adjectives above and below will help you.

مکزیکی، آمریکایی، برزیلی، ویتنامی، ایرانی
سلام! شما غذای تگزاسی می‌خورین؟
نه! من غذای تگزاسی نمی‌خورم!

Example: What is the most popular type of food in the class?

نوشتن   Writing Exercise

1. Use the vocabulary you have learned so far to write a short paragraph about yourself.

subject + object + verb

subject + adverb of time + object + verb

order of objects: direct object + obj of preposition + indirect object

order of adverbs: adverb of time + adv of manner + adv of place

من ناهار می‌خورم.

من امروز ناهار می‌خورم.

من امروز با دوستم ناهار می‌خورم.

من امروز با دوستم در رستوران البرز ناهار می‌خورم.

....
....
....
....

2. Use the vocabulary you have learned to write a conversation. Your conversation should have a setting (e.g. a restaurant, a classroom) and a short narrative. Write at least 20 sentences for your conversation.

حرف زدن   Speaking Activities

Homework:

Review the vocabulary and grammar for this lesson and think about how you would ask (and answer) the following questions. Practice them aloud until you can ask them fluidly.

~ At what time do you eat dinner?
~ Where do you eat dinner?
~ How many brothers do you have? How many sisters?
~ How many students are in your house?
~ Where are you from?
~ Where do you live?
~ Do you know where our professor lives?

In Class:

First watch the video (segment 9) with your instructor to learn some new greetings. Try them out on your classmates, then ask the questions listed above. Remember what they say so you can report it to the class later.

Language Games

1. The instructor will write a sentence on the board. The group with the most questions about that sentence will be the winner.

مثال : در تهران در یک رستوران ایرانی غذای مکزیکی می‌خورم.

2. The instructor writes 20 words on the board and then erases them. The groups (of three) have 45 seconds to write down as many of the words as they remember on a piece of paper. Misspelled words will not be counted.

3. **Red Rover Interview**: Your instructor will divide the class into two groups. Each group will write one question for each person in the other group. Each question must use at least two new vocabulary words. Then you will ask your questions of the other group and they must answer it on the spot. You can ask anything you want, so make it juicy!!

درس ششم
UNIT 6

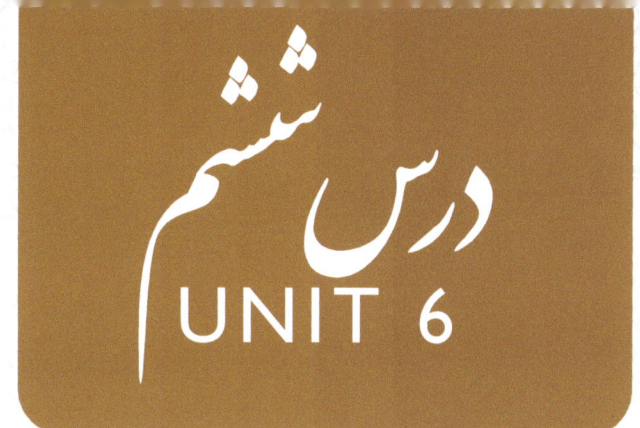

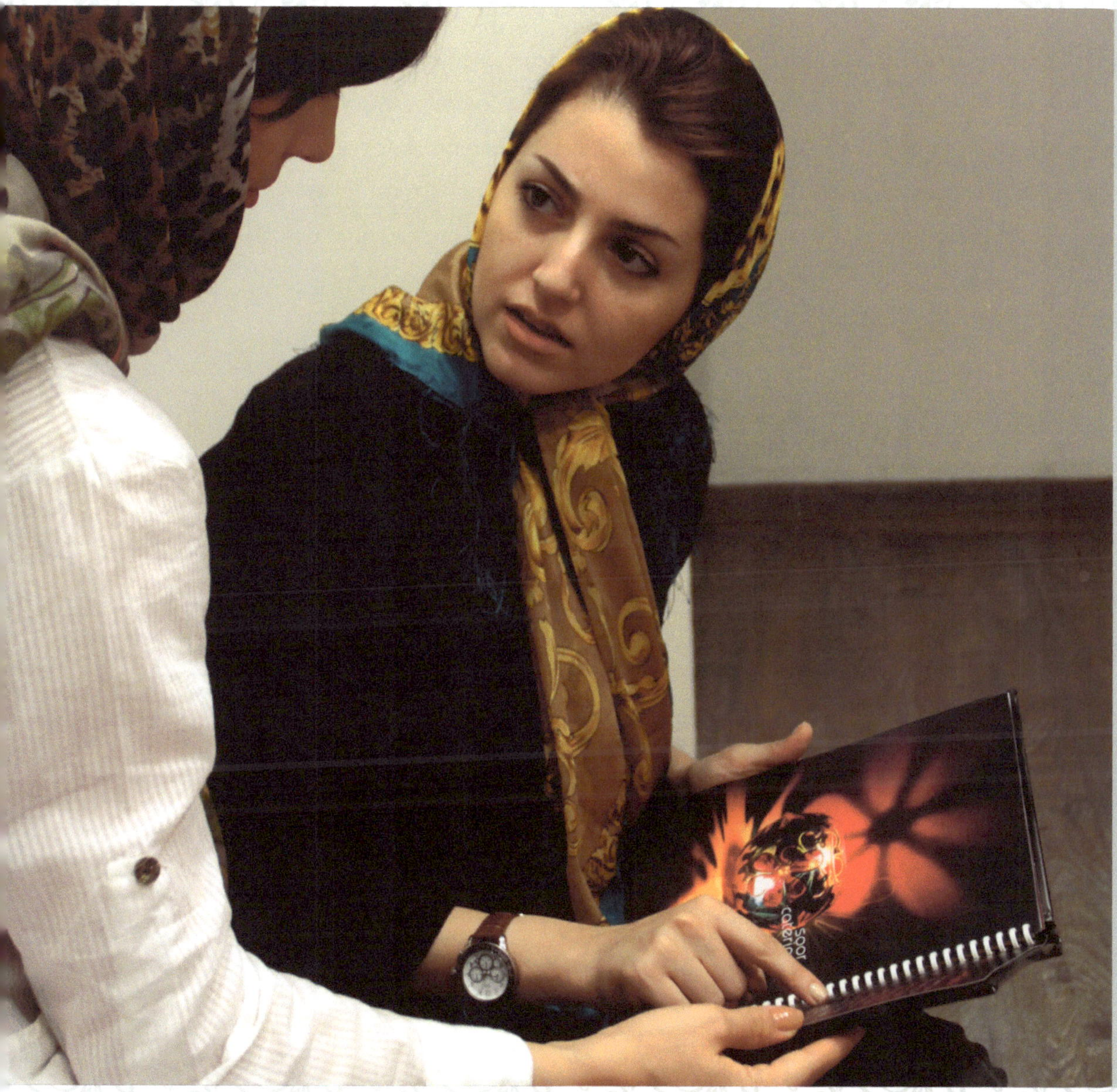

آ	ص
ب	ض
پ	ط
ت	ظ
ث	ع
ج	غ
چ	ف
ح	ق
خ	ک
د	گ
ذ	ل
ر	م
ز	ن
ژ	و
س	ه
ش	ی

Who is this? ایشون کی هستند؟

Cultural Note — یادداشت فرهنگی

مهمان‌نوازی Hospitality

Hospitality is a very important in Iranian culture. Accepting guests in one's home at any time and in any situation, inviting people over and serving delicious food with a smile and an open heart are considered fundamental to Iranian culture. Meeting up with old and new friends is one of the most common pastimes among Iranians.

Regular social gatherings constitute a cultural practice that forms close relationships among Iranians. Such relationships shape the social life of Iranians into a tightly woven network, which leaves little room for alone time. Although these relationships provide a warm and supportive social environment, intense social interactions consume a majority of people's time in everyday life. They create socio-cultural norms and rituals which one must follow in order to be accepted in the society. For example, inviting people to dinner is not just a hobby but rather the responsibility of families, and neglecting such a responsibility may cause drama or clashes among family members.

Short Conversations — گفتگوهای کوتاه

In class, listen to the audio files, repeat what you hear and try to fill in the blanks. At home repeat what you hear several times and try to follow the rhythm. Write two sentences in Persian about each conversation you hear (you can use made up names for the people who speak). During the next class time, you will work with a classmate to create a scenario that uses these expressions.

- ایشون .... هستن؟
- ایشون .... هستن.
- جوون ....! .... سالشونه؟
- .... سالشونه.

۱. ....
۲. ....

. این کیه؟
. این ....، سعید.
. ...؟
. اون ....

1. ....
2. ....

. ایشون کی ....؟
. دوستم، .... هستن.
. جدی؟ .... ؟ استاد ....؟
. بله.
. ایشون .... هستن؟! چه عالی!

1. ....
2. ....

| تشدید ّ | ...ص..ص... | ...ذ... | ...ع..ـعـ..ـع..ع... |

In this unit you will learn the symbol for doubling consonants and three more letters of the alphabet. Beginning in this unit, you will learn some letters that represent the same sound as letters you've learned before in previous units. This has to do with the origin of some words in Persian and it can make spelling tricky. However, this idea is nothing new for you. Consider the English words "fish" and "phase." How do you know "fish" starts with an "f" and "phase" with a "ph"? You memorized it! And that's what you'll have to do in Persian too.

Part 1: tashdid ﹷ

| تشکّر | امّا | شدّت | شدّ |

1. Listen to the audio file for file. ﹷ tashdid.

This symbol, called *tashdid*, is a pronunciation marker whose function is to double the length of a consonant in pronunciation. In Persian, doubled consonants are not written twice, but instead take tashdid. Do not associate the effect of tashdid with two identical, consecutive consonants in English, as in the word little. In Persian, doubling changes the pronunciation of the consonant over which it is written. Like other vocalization marks, tashdid is usually omitted in unvocalized texts, except where ambiguity might arise without it. In general, the reader is expected to know which words take tashdid, and to use context, if necessary, to guess. The difference between a single consonant and a doubled one is a question of length: a doubled consonant is pronounced and held for twice as long as a single one. Consider the English word "roommate." How would the word be pronounced if it were written roomate? Tashdid creates the former effect.

Tashdid is written like a tiny, rounded "w" above the consonant that it doubles. You'll notice that when a *zir* appears after a tashdid, it is written under the tashdid itself and not the letter.

2. Watch the video and write the following words.

کفّاش .... مدّت ....

تمدّن .... بچّه ....

3. Listen and check when the word you hear needs tashdid.

☐ ۴.   ☐ ۳.   ☐ ۲.   ☐ ۱.

☐ ۸.   ☐ ۷.   ☐ ۶.   ☐ ۵.

4. Circle ﹷ in the following texts. Report to your instructor how many ﹷ you identified in the text.

5. Listen and write the words you hear. Write a letter that includes "tashdid."

۱.   ۲.   ۳.   ۴.   ۵.

۶.   ۷.   ۸.   ۹.   ۱۰.

| صبر | مصر | حریص | حرص |

Part 2: sâd /s/   ‗ص‗ص‗

1. Listen to the audio file for ص sâd.

This letter represents the sound /s/ and is pronounced exactly like the letter س.

2. Writing ص : Watch the video and follow the instructions.

ص .... ص ....

3. Watch the video and write the following words.

صِدا ....

صورَت ....

صاف ....

مَنصور ....

صابون ....

مَخصوص ....

4. Circle the letter ص in the following text. Report to your instructor how many ص you identified in the text.

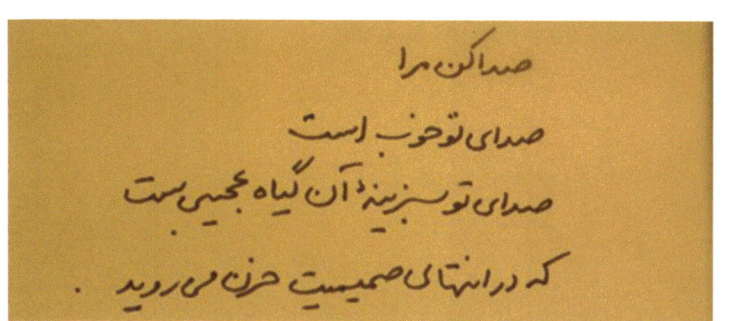

105   PERSIAN OF IRAN TODAY

5. Listen and write the words you hear. Write the /s/ sound with ص.

۱.   ۲.   ۳.   ۴.   ۵.   ۶.

۷.   ۸.   ۹.   ۱۰.   ۱۱.   ۱۲.

Part 3: zâl /z/ ___ذ___ | ذال | لذّت | لذیذ |

1. Listen to the audio file for file. ذ zâl.

This letter is pronounced exactly like ز, but it is written like د with a dot above it. Like د it does not connect to the following letter.

2. Watch the video and follow the instructions.

ذ ....

3. Watch the video and write the following words.

لذّت .... گذشته .... اذان ....

4. Listen and write the words you hear. Write "ذ" whenever you hear the /z/ sound.

۱.   ۲.   ۳.   ۴.   ۵.   ۶.

5. Circle the letter ذ in the following text. Report to your instructor how many ذ you identified in the text.

Part 4: eyn / ʾ /

عید	مُعَلِّم	رُبع	شُروع

ـع ـعـ ـعـ ع

1. Listen to the audio file for ع eyn.

This letter does not have an alphabetic equivalent in English, but you make its sound all the time. Try saying "uh-oh" several times and pay attention to the sound you make in between the two syllables. You make the same sound when you pronounce any word that begins with a vowel, such as our, if, it, I, on, up. Say these out loud, and pay attention to the "catch" in your throat as you pronounce the first vowel. In Persian, this sound is actually a consonant.

2. Watch the video and follow the instructions.

ـع ....

ـعـ ....

ـعـ ....

ع ....

3. Watch the video and write the following words.

عالی .... عِلم ....

مُعَلِّم .... شِعر ....

وَسیع .... شُروع ....

4. Listen and check when you hear the / ʾ / sound in the word.

۱. ☐   ۲. ☐   ۳. ☐   ۴. ☐   ۵. ☐

5. Circle the letter ع in the following text. Report to your instructor how many ع you identified in the text.

- برنامه های قهوه خانه هر شب پس از اذان مغرب با مراسم ترنا شروع و در فواصل هر برنامه ترنا اجرا می شود.
- ساعت ۱۸:۱۵ هر روز در فضای باز تئاترشهر معرکه پهلوانی توسط پهلوان رحمان اجرا می شود
- هر روز برنامه های پاتوق سنتی کودکان از ساعت ۱۷ با خیمه شب بازی شروع و تا ساعت ۱۹ با اجرای برنامه های مختلف ت

6. Listen and write the words you hear.

۱. ۲. ۳. ۴. ۵. ۶.

۷. ۸. ۹. ۱۰. ۱۱. ۱۲.

7. Connect the letters to form words.

۱. شَ + خ + ص + ی + یَ + ت ....

۲. مَ + ص + دَ + ر ....

۳. مُ + عَ + ل + لِ + م ....

۴. شَ + ف + ق ....

۵. آ + ف + ر + ی + ق + ا ....

۶. آ + ةَ + م + م + ی + یَ + ت ....

۷. مُ + عَ + د + دِ + ل ....

8. Listen to the following words. Fill in the missing letter or letters, then write the completed words on a separate piece of paper.

۱. نقاشی   ۲. ــدف   ۳. مــادل   ۴. مدت

۵. سرــت   ۶. ــدور   ۷. مرــوب   ۸. نجار

۹. صد____   ۱۰. قاره   ۱۱. ــواب   ۱۲. مهم

۱۳. ســادت   ۱۴. مقدس   ۱۵. ــربستان   ۱۶. فرــت

9. Read aloud the following words with your partner.

۴. عارِف	۳. مُهِمّ	۲. مادّه	۱. تَهیّه
۸. عالی	۷. عَصَبانی	۶. بَعد	۵. مُساعِدَت
۱۲. عَصر	۱۱. مُصادِره	۱۰. رَعد و بَرق	۹. مَعروف
۱۶. سُماق	۱۵. ذَلیل	۱۴. رِذالَت	۱۳. مُعاصِر
۲۰. آب مَعدَنی	۱۹. عَدَس	۱۸. سِرکه	۱۷. زَعفَران

10. Listen to the audio file and mark the word you hear.

قوری / گوری	۷	سوق / سوگ	۱
مگر / مقر	۸	گرم / قرن	۲
اگر / اقل	۹	نقاد / نگار	۳
گوش / قوچ	۱۰	قریب / گلیم	۴
شقاوت / شکایت	۱۱	قراین / گلایه	۵
مشق / مشک	۱۲	گاری / قاری	۶

11. Read the following words aloud with your partner. What do you notice about the relationship between the two columns?

شهرها	←	شَهر
موش‌ها	←	موش
مدرسه‌ها	←	مَدرِسه
درها	←	دَر
راه‌ها	←	راه
جوان‌ها/ جوانان	←	جَوان
دانشجوها/ دانشجویان	←	دانِشجو

PERSIAN OF IRAN TODAY

واژگان ۱ — Vocabulary 1

1. Listen to and learn these words. Translate the sentences. The spoken variations have been included in parentheses.

		English
۱. خانه‌ی شما	خانه شما این جاست؟ (خونه‌ی شما این جاست؟)	your house
۲. خانه‌اتان (خونه‌تون)	خانه‌اتان در این خیابان است؟ (خونه‌تون تو این خیابونه؟)	your house
۳. نمی‌دانم (نمی‌دونم)	نمی‌دانم خانه‌ی آنها کجاست. (نمی‌دونم خونه‌ی اونا کجاست.)	I do not know.
۴. شَب به خیر	شب شما به خیر!	good night
۵. روز به خیر	روزتان به خیر! (روزتون به خیر.)	good morning / day
۶. عالی	این شیرینی عالی است. (این شیرینی عالیه.)	excellent
۷. بُزُرگ	خانه آنها بزرگ است. (خونه اونا بزرگه.)	big
۸. کوچَک (کوچیک)	من یک برادر کوچک دارم. (من یه برادر کوچیک دارم.)	small
۹. کِتاب	او دو کتاب فارسی دارد. (اون دو تا کتاب فارسی داره.)	book
۱۰. مِداد	او سه مداد دارد. (اون سه تا مداد داره.)	pencil
۱۱. خُودکار	شما چهار خودکار داری؟ (شما چهار تا خودکار داری؟)	pen
۱۲. دَفتَر	آنها پنج دفتر دارند. (اونا پنج تا دفتر دارن.)	notebook
۱۳. پاک‌کن	پاک‌کن داری؟	eraser
۱۴. کیف	دو دفتر کوچک در کیفم دارم. (دو تا دفتر کوچیک تو کیفم دارم.)	bag
۱۵. میز	یک میز بزرگ در این کلاس است. (یه میز بزرگ تو این کلاسه.)	table
۱۶. صَندَلی	در این کلاس بیست صندلی کوچک هست. (تو این کلاس بیست تا صندلی کوچیک هست.)	chair
۱۷. بَچّه، کودَک	شش بچّه در خانه هستند. (شش تا بچّه تو خونه هستن.)	child
۱۸. جَوان	برادر تو جوان است؟ (برادر تو جوونه؟)	young
۱۹. پیر	پدر من پیر است. (پدر من پیره.)	old

۲۰. پسَر	آنها هفت پسر دارند. (اونا هفت تا پسر دارن.)	boy, son
۲۱. دُختَر	دختر من کوچک است. (دختر من کوچیکه.)	girl, daughter
۲۲. زیبا	یک خانه‌ی زیبا در این خیابان است. (یه خونه‌ی زیبا تو این خیابونه)	beautiful
۲۳. خوش تیپ	این مرد خوش‌تیپ برادرم است. (این مرد خوش‌تیپ برادرمه.)	handsome
۲۴. عراق	پدر دوستم یک خانه بزرگ در عراق دارد. (پدر دوستم یه خونه‌ی بزرگ تو عراق داره.)	Iraq
۲۵. عربستان سعودی	عربستان یک کشور مسلمان است. (Muslim) عربستان یه کشور مسلمونه.	Saudi Arabia
۲۶. چه کسی/ (کی؟)	چه کسی خسته است؟ (کی خسته است؟)	who

2. Listen to the audio file again. Based on what you hear, write the vowels on the example sentences. Now listen to the next audio file. Write the sentences you hear and translate them to English.

واژگان ۲   Vocabulary 2

3. Listen to and learn these words. Translate the sentences. The spoken variations have been included in parentheses.

۱. اتاق خواب	یک اتاق خواب بزرگ در خانه داریم. (... تو خونه ... .)	bedroom
۲. هال/ اتاق نشیمن	اینجا اتاق نشیمن است. (... نشیمنه.)	living room
۳. آشپزخانه (آشپزخونه)	آشپزخانه‌اشان کوچک است. (آشپزخونه‌شون کوچیکه.)	kitchen
۴. دستشویی- سرویس بهداشتی	ببخشید، دستشویی کجاست؟	restroom
۵. پله	در خانه‌اتان پله دارید؟ (تو خونه‌تون پله دارین؟)	stairs
۶. راهرو	این خانه سه راهروی بزرگ دارد. (این خونه سه تا راهروی بزرگ داره.)	hallway
۷. اتاق مهمان	در خانه اتاق مهمان نداریم. (تو خونه اتاق مهمون نداریم.)	guest room

4. Listen to the audio file again. Based on what you hear, write the vowels on the example sentences. Now listen to the next audio file. Write the sentences you hear and translate them to English.

Listening Comprehension / درک شنیدار

1. Watch the videos and answer the following questions in Persian.

1. What does Shayli show us in her house?
2. Where do you think she studies?
3. How does she feel about her apartment?
4. Who calls Shayli?
5. How does Shayli feel? What does her friend suggest she drink?
6. Where is Shayli going to go? With whom?

2. Listen to the audio file and answer the questions you hear in complete sentences in Persian.

۱. ....

۲. ....

۳. ....

۴. ....

۵. ....

Grammar Note / یادداشت دستوری

Ezâfe is a construction that marks a relationship between two words: nouns and other nouns, nouns and adjectives, or nouns and pronouns.

You actually already know how to create an *ezâfe* construction. Think back to possession. How did you make possessive phrases using pronouns? To review, fill in the following chart using pronouns to create possession. Make sure you read your answers aloud as you write them.

my book	کتاب من
his pencil	
our class	خودکار شما
their daughter	

You didn't write anything in between the noun and pronoun, but as you were reading them aloud, what did you say between them? …………………………………………………………………………

That /e/ sound marks ezâfe and it is usually how we indicate this kind of relationship between two words. Ezâfe can also mark possession between two nouns, similar to the English "of." How would you translate the following phrases?

Bâbak's bag	
	میز کلاس
University of Texas	

However, the ezâfe construction is not limited to possessive phrases. It is also used when we connect a noun and an adjective. Remember that in Persian the noun comes first and is followed by the adjective. Complete the following chart, connecting the noun and adjective in the proper order. Be sure to read your answers aloud and don't forget the /e/ sound in between the two words!

the big university	
the excellent book	
the little sister	
the old woman	

PERSIAN OF IRAN TODAY

Two Caveats

Now that you have a clearer idea of how to use *ezâfe*, keep the following rules in mind as you construct it.

1. In Persian, words can either end in vowels or consonants. Remember that a vowel is written at the end of the word with an *alef, vâv, ye, or a he* (which represents an /e/ sound). Look through your vocabulary lists from the last two lessons and separate the nouns according to their last letter, put words ending with vowels in the left column and words ending with consonants in the right column.

خانه	کتاب

This distinction is important because words that end with vowels act differently in *ezâfe* constructions. Specifically, when the first word in an *ezâfe* construction ends with a vowel, instead of just saying /e/ in between the two words, we actually write and pronounce a ی. You've already seen this construction in your most recent vocabulary list.

my house	khâne-ye man	خانه‌ی من

Because خانه ends with a vowel (/e/), we write a ی directly next to the ه without connecting it. If a word ends with an *alef* or a *vâv* (pronounced /u/), then we also write and pronounce a ی. However, if a word ends in ی, we don't write an additional ی. Consider the following example:

the big chair	sandali-ye bozorg	صندلی بزرگ

How would you translate the following phrases, keeping the rule you just learned in mind?

the small window	
their house	
the excellent university	

2. It is also possible to "stack" words in an ezâfe construction. However, if a pronoun is involved, remember that it always comes at the end! Look at the following example:

| my beautiful house | خانه‌ی زیبای من |

Can you write four examples of your own that use at least three words "stacked" in an ezâfe construction? Try to incorporate your new vocabulary as well.

١. ....
٢. ....
٣. ....
٤. ....

3. How would you translate the following phrases? Remember that ezâfe is not added to numbers.

	دو اتاق زیبا
	سه پنجره کوچک
	چهار مرد جوان

Ezâfe Practice

Determining where *ezâfe* goes is one of the biggest challenges to reading Persian. However, it is important because it demonstrates that you understand the meaning of the sentence. Practice by writing in the *ezâfe* markers (either the *zir* or *ye*).

١. خانه بزرگ ما پنج میز زیبا دارد.
٢. می‌دانم خواهر کوچک آنها کجاست.
٣. با اجازه شما یک آب میوه بزرگ می‌خورم.
٤. آقا دکتر، این دانشجو دانشجوی شما در کلاس فارسی دانشگاه تگزاس است؟
٥. کلاس ما در خیابان تهران است.

Listen to the audio file and check your answers.  Grammar 1

Grammar Exercises

1. Which of the sentences below could be the equivalent for the Persian phrase in the yellow box? Translate the other sentences. The vocabulary you may not know is given in the box.

روزِ خوبی داشته باشید!

vanilla	وانیل، وانیلی (adj)
ice cream	بَستَنی
milk	شیر
apple	سیب

How are you? ……………………………………..
Have a good day! ……………………………………..
Where are you from? ……………………………………..
She has two brothers. ……………………………………..
I do not have an apple. ……………………………………..
I like vanilla ice cream. ……………………………………..
My brother's name is Bahram. ……………………………………..
She drinks milk. ……………………………………..

Memorize the phrase روز خوبی داشته باشید! for future use!

2. Add nouns or adjectives to the following words to make phrases. Then make sentences with each phrase.

……………………………	خانه ……………………
……………………………	مداد ……………………
……………………………	کیف ……………………
……………………………	مرد ……………………
……………………………	فوتبال ……………………
……………………………	زن ……………………

3. Fill in the blanks with appropriate words. Add ezafe wherever necessary.

۱. اسم من ساراست . من .... هستم اما با پدر و مادرم در اصفهان زندگی می‌کنم.

۲. ما یک خانه .... در اصفهان داریم. جا نداریم.

۳. من .... دانشگاه اصفهان هستم و در دانشگاه چهار دوست خوب دارم. .... دختر هستند.

۴. من و برادرم آب میوه ....

۵. (نمی‌دونم .... و .... شما کجا است. - این‌جاست. توی کیفمه؟)

۶. این زن .... استاد فیزیک ما است.

۷. در این کلاس چند .... و .... هست؟

4. Fill in the blanks with the correct form of the verbs "to be," "to eat," "to live," and "to have."

۱. من و دوستم شیرینی شکلاتی ....

۲. این چهار مرد در اصفهان ....

۳. شما و برادرتان ماشین .... ؟

۴. او شب‌ها چای ....

5. Listen to the audio files and answer the following questions in Persian.

Grammar 3

1. Who lives in the house?

2. How many خواب اتاق are there in the house?

3. Who shares one bedroom?

4. How many guest rooms are there in the house?

5. How are the windows in the bedrooms?

6. Where does the family dine?

7. Where are the bathrooms?

Writing exercise نوشتن

1. Use the vocabulary you have learned so far to write a short paragraph about your house., or find a picture related to a house and describe the house.

Speaking Activities حرف زدن

In Class:
Try to describe your surroundings to your classmates. Say things like "This book is big!" Or "This is a big book!"

For Homework:
Review the vocabulary on p.66 and the grammar note on ezâfe and think of how you would ask your classmates the following questions. Practice them aloud several times so you can ask them fluidly in class. Think about how you might answer these questions and be sure you know how to say "I don't know."

~ Where is your house?

~ Is your house big?

~ Is this your book?

~ Do you have a son or daughter? What is his/her name?

~ Does your brother have a small notebook?

~ Is there a pen in your bag?

~ Do you have a big table in your house?

~ Who in Hollywood is very handsome? Pretty?

~ Who in this class knows three languages?

~ Do you live in a house or an apartment (آپارتمان)?

~ How many bedrooms and bathrooms does it have?

~ Do you eat dinner in the kitchen or the living room?

In Class:
Now practice with your classmates. Ask your neighbors the questions you practiced. Pay attention to what they say, as your instructor may ask you to report what you've learned to the class. Be sure to thank your classmates!

Classroom Activities — فعالیت‌های پیشنهادی برای کلاس

Cribs: Work with a partner. Your instructur will give each of you a different picture of a house. You must describe your house to your partner and s/he will draw it. Then switch roles. Your partner will describe his/her picture while you draw it. Do all of this without looking at your partner's picture!

The following words will be useful as you describe your pictures:

above	اتاق‌ها بالایِ آشپزخانه هستند.	بالا
to the left of	آشپزخانه سمتِ چپِ اتاق نشیمن است.	سَمتِ چَپ
to the right of	دستشویی سمتِ راستِ پله است.	سَمتِ راست

برای استاد: جمله‌های بالا را برای دانشجویان بخوانید و توجه آنها را به «اضافه» بعد از حرف اضافه جلب کنید..

درس هفتم
UNIT 7

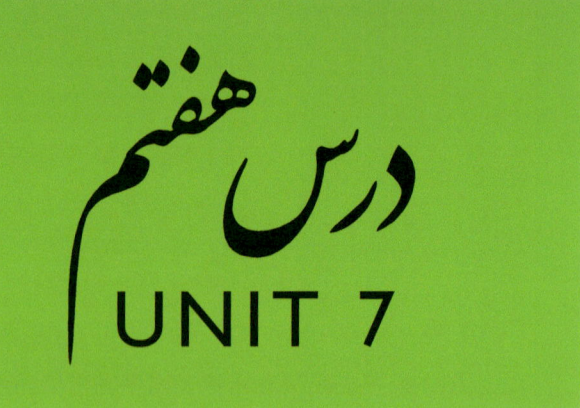

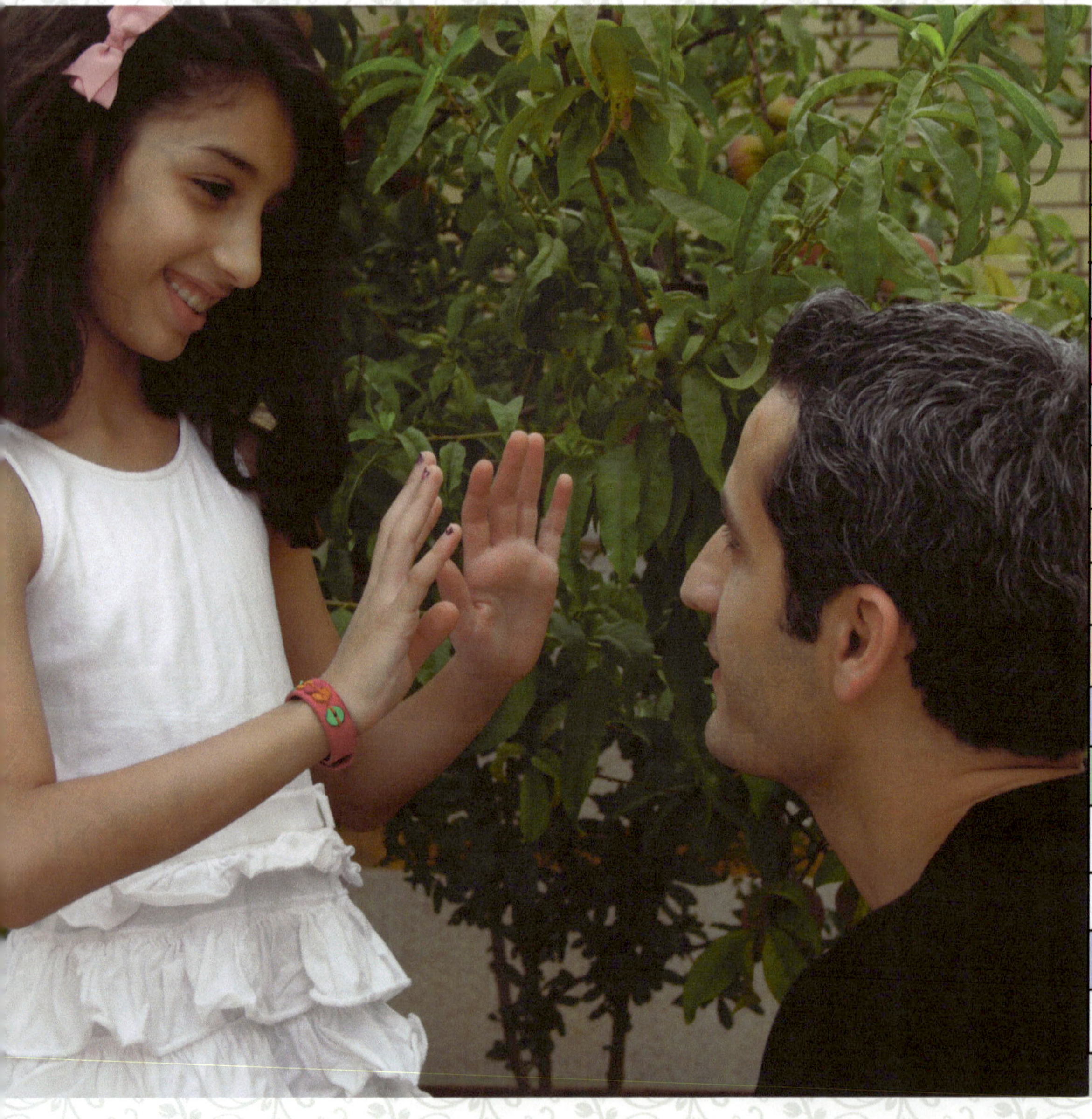

آ	ص
ب	ض
پ	ط
ت	ظ
ث	ع
ج	غ
چ	ف
ح	ق
خ	ک
د	گ
ذ	ل
ر	م
ز	ن
ژ	و
س	ه
ش	ی

How old are you? چند سالتونه؟

Cultural Note — یادداشت فرهنگی

مزاحم‌تون نمی‌شم! I don't want to bother you

Iranians are very comfortable asking and responding to questions that may be considered too personal in Western societies. In everyday conversation, Iranians often discuss and ask about one's weight, salary, religion, age, and political views. Making comments about someone's weight is not considered disrespectful, and people might give each other advice on how to lose weight or get in better shape.

While these kinds of personal questions are considered culturally appropriate, in other contexts people are indirect when responding to requests. Iranians often use ambiguous comments or indirect phrases to communicate their needs or respond to a request. In this context, being blunt is not considered an appropriate cultural practice in Iran. For example, if someone asks you if you would like tea, you might answer, "No, thanks. I don't want to bother you." نه ممنون نمی‌خوام به زحمت بیافتین, which is actually used to accept the tea.

Short Conversations گفتگوهای کوتاه

In class, listen to the audio files, repeat what you hear and try to fill in the blanks. At home repeat what you hear several times and try to follow the rhythm. Write at least two sentences in Persian about each **conversation**. You can use made up names for the people who are talking. During the next class time, you will work with a classmate to create a scenario that uses these expressions.

- چند سالتونه؟
- بیست و .... سال. شما .... سالتونه؟
- من .... سالمه.

1. ....
2. ....

- .... هستند؟
- بله.
- .... ؟
- بیست سالشه.

1. ....
2. ....

- مادربزرگ .... ؟
- .... سالشونه.
- ماشاالله! .... چند سالشونه؟
- .... پنجاه و .... سالشه.

1. ....
2. ....

- ببخشید، ممکنه .... چند سالتونه؟
- بله، بنده .... سال دارم.

1. ....
2. ....

...ط....	...ض...ض...	...ح...ح...	...ث...ث...

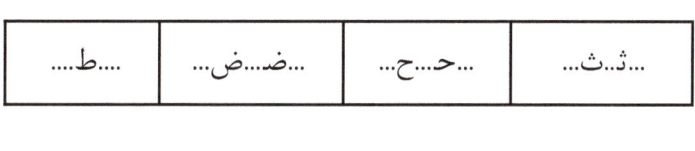

ثریّا	مثال	باعث

Part 1: se /s/ ___ث___ ث___

1. Listen to the audio file for ث se.

The letter se is pronounced exactly like the letter س (which marks three letters that you have learned representing the same sound). It is written like ب but with three dots above in an upside-down v-shape.

2. Watch the video and follow the instructions.

ث .... ژ ....

3. Watch the video and write the following words.

لَثه .... مِثال ....
مُثَلَّث .... کَثیف ....

4. Find and circle the letter ث in the following text (in the titles). Report to your instructor how many ث you identified in the text.

5. Listen and write the words you hear. Use ث when you hear /s/ sound.

۱.   ۲.   ۳.   ۴.   ۵.

۶.   ۷.   ۸.   ۹.   ۱۰.

Part 2: he /h/ ‎ـحـ ح

روح	صبح	سحر	حرف

1. Listen to the audio file for ح he.

The letter *he* is pronounced exactly like ه, which you learned earlier. It is written like ج, but without dots.

2. Watch the video and follow the instructions.

ح .... حـ

3. Watch the video and write the following words.

حَرف .... حِیوان .... صُبح ....

صُحبَت .... صُبحانه .... صَفحِه ....

4. Listen and check when you hear the /h/ sound in the word.

١. ☐   ٢. ☐   ٣. ☐   ٤. ☐   ٥. ☐

5. Circle the letter ح in the following texts. Report to your instructor how many ث you identified in the text.

در پشت صحنه برنامه موفق رادیو

حرف خوب زدن، خوب حرف زدن

این شب‌ها، برنامه‌ای در شبکه آموزش (کانال ۷) گل کرده، برنامه‌ای در آخر شب‌ها که محور آن متن خوانی است، نام آن هم بر همین موضوع تکیه دارد «رادیو۷»، این برنامه حالا شاید محبوب‌ترین برنامه آخر شبی تمام شبکه‌های سیما باشد...

6. Listen and write the words you hear. Use ح when you hear the /he/ sound.

١.   ٢.   ٣.   ٤.   ٥.

٦.   ٧.   ٨.   ٩.   ١٠.

Part 3: zâd /z/ ــضــض ــ

| حوض | مریض | بعضی | ضمیر |

1. Listen to the audio file for ض zâd.

This letter represents the sound ز.

2. Watch the video and follow the instructions.

ض .... ضـ ....

3. Watch the video and write the following words.

فَضا .... ضَمیر ....

توضیح .... مَریض ....

ضَرَر .... مَضمون ....

4. Circle the letter ض in the following text.. Report to your instructor how many ض you identified in the text.

5. Listen and write the words you hear.

۵.   ۴.   ۳.   ۲.   ۱.

| طوطی | وطن | حیاط |

Part 4: tâ /t/ ‏ـط‏

1. Listen to the audio file for ط tâ.

The letter tâ represents the same sound as the letter ت .

2. Watch the video and follow the instructions.

ط ....

3. Watch the video and write the following words.

طول .... مطلق .... فقط .... خط ....

4. Write the words in the appropriate box.

بُزُرگ، فَرَط، ضَعَف، سَعادَت، قرنطینه، مَخصوص، اِضافی، مُعَلِّم، باطری، اِصلاحات، ضایِع، مَضروب، اَذان، سَعی، صِداقَت، مُطلَق، تَعارُف، مُصالِحه، اِطِّلاع، تَفَکُّر، اَوَّلین، اِجازه، طلا، گُذاشت

ذ	ع	ص	ض	تشدید ـّـ	ط

5. Listen and write the words you hear. Use ط when you hear the /t/ sound.

۱. .... ۲. .... ۳. .... ۴. .... ۵. ....

6. Circle the letter ط in the following text. Report to your instructor how many ط you identified in the text.

[هنرهای سنتی]
همطراز با شکوه هنر خاتم
به بهانهٔ درگذشت استاد غلامرضا روزی‌طلب

6. Read the following words aloud with your partner.

۴. قَطَر	۳. واحِد	۲. مَطلَب	۱. اِستِحقاق
۸. مُضطَرِب	۷. حالا	۶. اَطلَس	۵. حُدود
۱۲. حَبیب	۱۱. ضایِعه	۱۰. فَرض	۹. حُقِّه
۱۶. ضَعیف	۱۵. وَحید	۱۴. مَضروب	۱۳. مُضایِقه
۲۰. ضایِعه	۱۹. اِنقِضا	۱۸. ضَعف	۱۷. حِزب

واژگان Vocabulary 1

1. Listen to and learn these words. Translate the sentences. The spoken variations have been included in parentheses.

۱. می‌خوریم	بستنی می‌خوریم. (instructors can introduce a few "food" words)	we eat, we drink
۲. به	به خانه‌ام در خیابان پنجم می‌روم. (می‌رم خونه‌ام تو خیابون پنجم.)	to
۳. به ... می‌رَوَم (می‌رم)	به دانشگاه می‌روم. (می‌رم دانشگاه.)	I go to
۴. خَسته	آن هفت پسر خسته هستند. (اون هفت تا پسر خسته‌ان.)	tired
۵. تِشنه‌ام (تشنَّمه)	آن دختر تشنه است. (اون دختر تشنَّست)	I am thirsty.
۶. گُرسِنه‌ام (گرسنَمه)	آن هشت گرسنه به یک رستوران ایتالیایی می‌روند. (اون هشت تا پسر گرسنه می‌رن یه رستوران ایتالیایی.)	I am hungry.
۷. خوشحال	آن نه دختر خوشحال هستند. (اون نه تا دختر خوشحالن.)	happy
۸. ناراحَت	آن ده پسر و دختر ناراحت هستند. (اون ده تا پسر و دختر ناراحتن.)	sad
۹. عَصَبانی	آن پسر جوان عصبانی است. (اون پسر جوون عصبانیه.)	angry
۱۰. مریض	حالم خوب نیست. مریضم.	sick
۱۱. تنبل	این پسر تنبل دوست من است. (این پسر تنبل دوست منه.)	lazy
۱۲. (اینجا گرمه، گرمه)/(گرممه)	(شما گرمتونه؟)	it's warm in here, it's warm, I'm hot
۱۳. سرد/ (سَردَمه)	(ما سردمونه.)	cold/ I'm cold, It's cold

I work	در تهران کار می کنم. (تو تهران کار می کنم.)	۱۴. کار می کُنَم
restaurant	در رستوران کار می کنم. (تو رستوران کار می کنم.)	۱۵. رِستوران
kabob	در رستوران کباب می خورید؟ (تو رستوران کباب می خورین؟)	۱۶. کَباب
with your permission	با اجازه‌ی شما چای می خورم.	۱۷. با اجازه‌ی شما
to be from somewhere	اهل تاجیکستان هستم.	۱۸. اَهلِ
but	ایرانی هستم اما فارسی بلد نیستم.	۱۹. اَمّا
library	من در کتاب‌خانه کار می کنم. (من تو کتاب خونه کار می کنم.)	۲۰. کتاب‌خانه
dormitory	خسته‌ام و به خوابگاه می روم. (خسته‌ام و می رم به خوابگاه.)	۲۱. خوابگاه

2. Listen to the audio file again. Based on what you hear, write the vowels on the example sentences.
Now listen to the next audio file. Write the sentences you hear and translate them to English.

واژگان   Vocabulary 2

3. Listen to and learn these words. Translate the sentences.
The spoken variations have been included in parentheses.

ten	ده رستوران در این خیابان هست. (ده رستوران تو این خیابون هست.)	۱. ده
twenty	تهران بیست دانشگاه دارد. (تهران بیست تا دانشگاه داره.)	۲. بیست
thirty	سی خانه‌ی بزرگ در اینجا هست. (سی خونه‌ی بزرگ اینجا هست.)	۳. سی
forty	چهل کودک در خیابان هستند.	۴.۴ چِهِل
fifty	پنجاه دختر و پسر جوان در این کلاس هستند. (پنجاه دختر و پسر جوون تو این کلاس هستن.)	۵. پَنجاه
sixty	آمریکا شصت دانشگاه عالی دارد. (آمریکا شصت تا دانشگاه عالی داره.)	۶. شَصت
seventy	این دانشگاه هفتاد استاد دارد. (این دانشگاه هفتاد تا استاد داره.)	۷. هَفتاد
eighty	ما هشتاد کتاب فارسی داریم. (ما هشتاد تا کتاب فارسی داریم.)	۸. هَشتاد
ninety	این دانشگاه نود کلاس دارد. (این دانشگاه نود تا کلاس داره.)	۹. نَوَد
a hundred/a thousand	تهران صد رستوران خوب دارد. (تهران صد تا رستوران خوب داره.)	۱۰. صَد/ هِزار

4. Listen to the audio file again. Based on what you hear, write the vowels on the example sentences.
Now listen to the next audio file. Write the sentences you hear and translate them to English.

Listening Comprehension درک شنیدار

Watch video one and answer the following questions in complete sentences **in Persian.**

1. Tonight Shayli is going to her friend's birthday party. What is her friend's name?
2. How old will Shayli's friend be tonight?
3. Where is the birthday party?
4. What is the address?

Watch video two and answer the following questions in complete sentences **in Persian.**

۵. مهدی و وحید اهل کجا هستند؟

۶. وحید در کجا زندگی می‌کند؟

Watch video three and answer the following questions in complete sentences **in Persian.**

7. What does Raha call Vahid?
8. Why do you think she does this (answer this part in English)?
9. What does Raha say when she wants to say goodbye?

How does Vahid answer?

Watch video four and answer the following questions in complete sentences **in Persian.**

10. Transcribe the phrase that Mr. Ja'fari uses to thank Mr. Hashemi for the tea.

Grammar Note — یادداشت دستوری

More on the verb "to be."

At this point, you have been using the present-tense conjugation of the verb "to be" in your speaking and writing. Although the conjugations you have learned are used often, a condensed version of the present-tense of "to be" is also used frequently. You have actually already used this version in your speaking practice. Consider the following example:

You know that خوب means "good" or "well" and خوبم means "I am well." What have we added to the end of خوب to mark "I am"? …………………………

That ـَم or اَم (in fact the sound /am/) should look familiar to you. It is the same ending we use for هستم, which you know means "I am." We can, therefore, just use the personal endings of the present tense of "to be" to represent the entire conjugation. We add these endings directly to nouns and adjectives. In Persian grammar books, you see the column in green as the condensed form of verb "to be." However, this column in fact shows the pronunciation of the form when it attaches to a noun or an adjective. It is the the final sound of the original word that determines the spelling of the entire word. For example, when any of the short forms comes after a consonant, the yellow column is used at the end of the word. Complete the left coloumn of the chart with the correct pronoun form for each person.

to be happy The final sound is /l/.	How the form of the short form of "to be" when it comes after a consonants	the sound of the short form of "to be"		verb "to be"
خوشحالم	ـَم	am	اَم	هستم
	ـی	i	ای	هستی
	است	ast	است	است
	یم	im	ایم	هستیم
	ید	id	اید	هستید
	ـَند	and	اَند	هستند

Why do you think that there is no way to apply this new concept to است؟ …………………………
…………………………

Hopefully you figured out that we don't apply this concept to the conjugation است because it does not take a personal ending, so we just stick to the full conjugation for the third-person singular (he/she) in written form, although است itself becomes ه or ـه in spoken form. This construction is used in both writing and speaking, but it is more common in the spoken form. Make sure you know the spoken version by filling in the following chart.

مثال Example	شکل کوتاه فعل بودن در گفتاری	ضمیر شخصی
		من
		تو
خوبه	ـه/ه	اون
		ما
	اید/این	شما
		اونا

One final note: Do you remember when you were learning ezâfe and you discovered that words that end with vowels function differently in *ezâfe* constructions? Nouns and adjectives that end with ه (pronounced /e/) also require a special rule in this case. You've already seen this in your vocabulary lists.

I am thirsty	تشنه‌ام	thirsty	تشنه

What is placed in between the م and the word تشنه? This is a spelling convention that keeps all of the pieces of this construction clear. Notice that the *alef* is written directly next to the ه but it does not connect to it. We use this spelling convention for all of these kinds of conjugations. Complete the chart to practice.

â sound	i sound	e sound	SUB.P
زیبایم	ایرانی‌ام	تشنه‌ام	من
زیبایی			تو
زیباست			اون
زیباییم			ما
زیبایید			شما
زیبایند			اونا

In class you will work on pronunciation for this concept. Use the following space to make notes about the pronunciation.

....
....
....

Transform the following sentences, using the condensed version of the verb "to be."

۱. قهوه‌ی من گرم است. ....

۲. گرسنه هستید. ....

۳. خوش‌حال هستند. ....

۴. ناراحت هستیم. ....

۵. در رستوران هستی. ....

Simple and Compound Verbs

	آمَدَن - آ
	من
	تو
می‌آیَد (می‌آد)	او (اون)
	ما
	شما
	آنها (اونا)

Verb: آمَدَن (to come). Use your knowledge of regular present-tense conjugation to complete the following chart.
*Present-tense stem (written): آی
*Present-tense stem (spoken): آ

	رَفتَن - رو
	من
	تو
می‌رَوَد (می‌ره)	او (اون)
	ما
	شما
	آنها (اونا)

Verb: رَفتَن (to go). Use your knowledge of regular present-tense conjugation to complete the following chart.
*Present-tense stem (written): رَو
*Present-tense stem (spoken): ر

Every time you learn a verb, get into the habit of charting it out like you have just done. This is a useful activity that will help you review the conjugation practices and will make it easier to remember how to use these verbs in the future. Here are the completed chatrs for "آمَدَن" and "رَفتَن". In these charts the verbs have come in one single column. Choose the style you are more comfortable with when you make your charts.

آمَدَن - آ

می‌آیم	میام	من
می‌آیید/ می‌آیی	میاین/ میای	شما/ تو
می‌آیند / می‌آید	میان / میاد	ایشون/ او (اون)
می‌آییم	میایم	ما
می‌آیید	میاین	شما
می‌آیند	می‌آن	آن‌ها (اونا)

رَفتَن - رو

می‌روم	میرم
می‌روید/ می‌روی	میرین/ میری
می‌روند/ می‌رود	میرن/ میره
می‌رویم	میریم
می‌روید	میرین
می‌روند	میرن

A note about the spoken form: The verbs "to go" and "to come" in Persian are different than the verbs you learned before because in their conjugations both the stem and the ending change in the spoken form. However, these verbs of motion are also special because they affect the sentence structure when spoken. In your vocabulary list for this lesson, you'll see the following sample sentence:

| I go home. | به خانه می‌رَوَم. |

You'll notice that the verb comes at the end of this written sentence. We must also write the word به in order to indicate our destination. However, in spoken Persian, the destination often immediately *follows* the verb. So the sample sentence above would become

| I go home. | میرَم خونه. |

Note that we've used the spoken variation of "I go" and "house," plus we have changed the structure of the sentence. We also don't need to use به when speaking, although it is necessary when written.

Compound Verbs

The Persian verb system is unique because of the presence of compound verbs. These verbs consist of two parts: a simple verb and a noun. These two pieces work together to convey a singular meaning. The most common simple verb in these combinations is the verb کردن, so it will be useful to memorize its conjugation well. To get started, complete the following chart:

Present-tense stem: کُن

کَردَن - کُن

من	
تو	
او (اون)	می‌کند (می‌کنه)
ما	
شما	
آنها (اونا)	می‌کنند (می‌کنن)

In your vocabulary list for this lesson, you'll see that you learned one example of a compound verb:

| I live. | زندگی می‌کنم |

Notice that when a compound verb is conjugated, the verbal component remains completely separate from the noun. That is, the می is affixed to the verbal part of the compound verb and not the noun part.

Grammar Exercises

1. Translate the following sentences into English.

۱. نمی‌دانم خانه‌ی برادرتان کجاست.
۲. مادرتان نان و پنیر می‌خورد؟
۳. خواهرم در آمریکا زندگی می‌کند. او فارسی بلد نیست.
۴. سلام آقای دکتر، خوب نیستم. ورزش دوست ندارم. شیرینی و بستنی می‌خورم.
۵. کجا می‌روید؟
۶. می‌روم رستورانِ دانشگاه. گرسنه‌ام.
۷. من می‌روم خانه. خسته‌ام.

2. Translate the following sentences into Persian.

   1. My brother does not eat bread. He does not like bread.

   2. Where does your sister live?

   3. I like your friend. Is she hungry?

   4. Are you tired? We will go home.

   5. Where is your father? Does he live in Texas?

3. Write sentences with each word. Use at least one *ezâfe* in each sentence.

۱. کلاس ....
۲. مادر ....
۳. شما ....

4. Use the vocabulary from this lesson to fill in the blanks in the sentences below. The sentences in parentheses are in the spoken form.

۱. دوست شما .... تهران است؟ - بله، او تهرانی است.

۲. .... این رستوران خوب است.

۳. پدرم .... دوست ندارد، آب می‌خورد.

۴. (کجا .... ؟ . ... خونه.)

۵. .... ای؟ آب می‌خوری؟

۶. من آمریکایی هستم .... دانشگاهم در اروپا است.

۷. (اینجا گرم است. من ....)

۸. در این رستوران .... ؟ - بله.

۹. کجا .... می‌کنی؟ - در مادرید اسپانیا.

5. Listen to what Ali says and answer the following questions in complete sentences in Persian.

Grammar 1

۱. علی چند سال دارد و اهل کجاست؟ ....

۲. او کجا زندگی می‌کند؟ ....

۳. با کی زندگی می‌کند؟ ....

۴. کجا ناهار و شامش را می‌خورد؟ ....

5. What is his room like? ....

6. How does he get to school? ....

A New Verb

The verb "to say" will add depth to your abilities in Persian by allowing you to communicate your own ideas and the ideas of other people as well. Use your knowledge of present-tense verb conjugations to complete the chart below. The spoken variation is included in the parentheses. Listen to the audio file to check your answers.

Grammar 2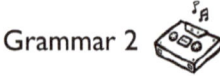

	گُفتَن - گو
می‌گویم (می‌گم)	من
	تو
	او (اون)
	ما
می‌گویید (می‌گین)	شما
می‌کنند (می‌کنن)	آنها (اونا)

check your answers again!

		گُفتَن - گوی - گ
میگم	می‌گویم	
میگین / میگی	می‌گویید / می‌گویی	
میگن / میگه	می‌گویند / می‌گوید	
میگیم	می‌گوییم	
میگین	می‌گویید	
میگن	می‌گویند	

Read the following sentences with the verb "to say" and answer the questions below.

> ۱. دوستم می‌گوید هر روز به کتاب‌خانه می‌رود.
> (دوستم می‌گه هر روز می‌ره کتاب‌خونه.)
> ۲. می‌گویند آنجا گرم است. (می‌گن اونجا گرمه.)

1. What do you notice about the sentence structure when this verb is involved? This structure is similar to sentences with what other verb that you know?

....

....

2. How do you think this verb is being used in the second sentence? (Hint: Do we necessarily know who the subject is?)

....

....

> Fill in the blank using the appropriate present-tense conjugation of the verb "to say" and translate the sentences into English.

۱. من و مادرم .... این رستوران خیلی خوب است.

۲. خانواده‌اش .... رفتن به کتاب‌خانه کار خوبی است.

....

۳. .... وقتی در خوابگاه زندگی می‌کنید زندگی راحت است.

....

۴. معلم به ما .... تکلیف ما چیست.

....

۵. شما به من .... خانه‌تان کجاست؟

In Class:
Take five minutes to write a sentence that the people below would normally say. Then work with a partner and say your sentences using گفتن and اونا / اون / ایشون. Your partner must guess the person you're describing using a complete sentence. Make sure your sentences are appropriate to the specific people you are describing, otherwise your partner won't be able to guess. Look at the example below.

- ایشون میگن ورزش کردن کار خوبیه.

- دکتر میگه وزرش کردن کار خوبیه.

- درسته!

استاد ....

معلم ....

دکتر ....

وکیل ....

مادر و پدر ....

خواهر ....

Writing exercise نوشتن

Write a paragraph about yourself. Try to talk about where you are from, what you do, how old you are, where you live, how many siblings you have, where they live and how old they are, etc.

Speaking Activities حرف زدن

In Class:
Review the vocabulary on page 110 and 111 about telling someone how you feel, then play charades with one of your classmates. Make a face indicating how you feel and your partner will guess the emotion in Persian.

Homework:
Review the vocabulary and grammar note and think about how you would ask the following questions. Practice them aloud several times so you can ask them fluidly in class, and think about how you might answer these questions yourself.

~ Where do you live?
~ Where does your mother live? Where does your father live?
~ Do you go to your mother's house?
~ Are the students in this class lazy?!!
~ Is this room cold or warm?

In Class:

Now, practice with your classmates. Ask your neighbors the questions above. Pay attention to what they say, as your instructor may ask you to report what you've learned to the class. Be sure to thank your classmates.

Introducing a new word:

وقتی (وختی)

This word means "when," but it is not a question word. Look at the examples below:

وقتی عصبانی هستم حرف نمی‌زنم.

Talk with your classmates and find out...

...what they do when they are sad.

....what they do when they are angry.

...what they do when they are happy.

Language Games

1. **Sentence Charades:** Divide into small groups of 3 or 4. Work with your group to write 5 to 10 sentences on small pieces of paper. Fold the papers in half. A student from another group will select one of the sentences and act it out. The group has a minute and a half to guess the sentence. Each sentence properly guessed is worth 10 points. Using any non-Persian words will cause your team to lose one point! Before acting out your sentence, you may indicate the number of words and prepositions on the board with lines and circles.

مثال: من و برادرم به دانشگاه می‌رویم

The person who acts will fill in each blank when the group mentions each word.

2. **Circle Sentences:** You, your teacher, and your classmates should form a circle. The teacher begins by pointing at the student next to her and describing her. For example:

این دختر خسته مریمه.

Now the student whom the teacher just described, points to the next student and uses an adjective to describe him or her.

Consider using the following adjectives: tired, hungry, thirsty, beautiful, sad, angry, happy, Iranian, sick, lazy, etc.

درس هشتم
UNIT 8

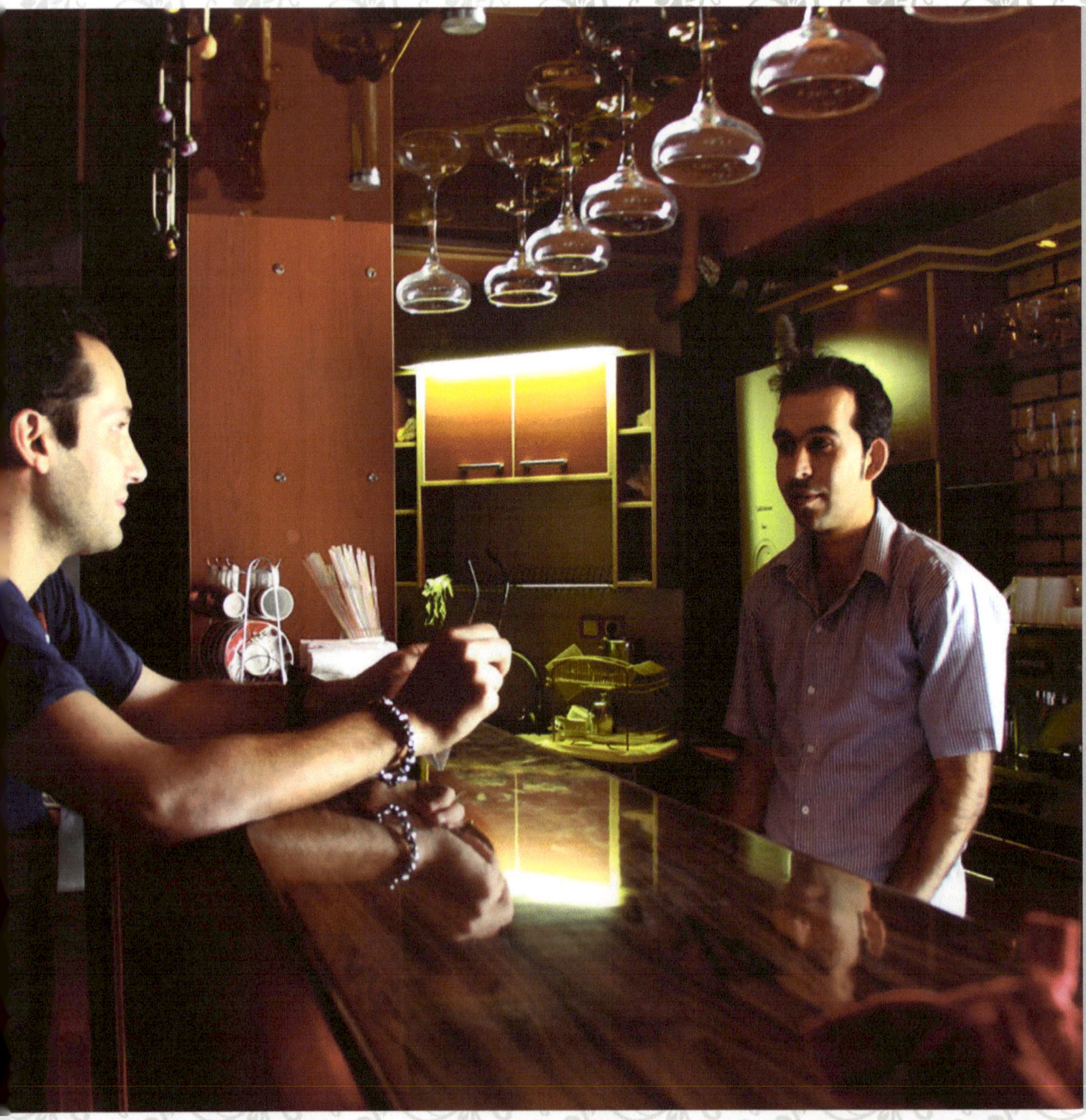

صبح‌تون به خیر!
خوش آمدید!

Good morning!
Welcome!

Cultural Note — یادداشت فرهنگی

صبح‌تون به خیر، خوش آمدید.

Being an early bird is a valuable trait according to Iranian culture. There are a number of Iranian proverbs and poems that suggest that waking up early in the morning may help one have a successful day. "سحرخیز باش تا کامروا شوی" /sahar khiz bâsh tâ kâmravâ bâshi/ is one such proverb that elderly people use to give advice to young people. It means "wake up early to be successful". However, Iranian culture does not necessarily value promptness! Iranians does not usually stress setting an exact time for a meeting or plans. It is not uncommon for an event, even a very formal gathering, to start half an hour or an hour late.

صبح به خیر!   ظهر به خیر!   عصر به خیر!   شب به خیر!

PERSIAN OF IRAN TODAY

Short Conversations گفتگوهای کوتاه

In class, listen to the audio files, repeat what you hear and try to fill in the blanks. At home repeat what you hear several times and try to follow the rhythm. Write at least two sentences in Persian about each **picture.** During the next class time, you will work with a classmate to create a scenario that uses these expressions.

. سلام، صبح .... به خیر!
. سلام، .... به خیر. حال‌تون .... ؟
. ...، شما چه طورین؟
. ...، خوبم.

۱. ....
۲. ....

. سلام، ظهرتون به .... خیلی .... آمدید.

۱. ....
۲. ....

. ... به خیر. .... خوبه؟
. بله، ....

۱. ....
۲. ....

شب‌تون به خیر. چی ....؟

۱. ....

۲. ....

In class, work with a classmate to create a scenario that uses these expressions.

شب به خیر! (used at the time of sleeping)

روزتون به خیر! (anytime before evening)

روزتون خوش! (when leaving)

شب‌تون خوش! (usually when leaving)

...غ...غ..غ...غ....	...ظ...

In this unit, you will learn the last two letters.

Part 1: *gheyn* /gh/ ‌ـغ‌ ‌ـغـ‌ ‌غـ‌ ‌غ‌ | داغ | جیغ | مغلوب | غار

1. Listen to the audio file for غ *gheyn*.

This letter is pronounced exactly like ق, which you learned in Unit 5. You will have to memorize the spelling of any words containing ق or غ. Note that this letter is written exactly like ع, but with a dot above it.

2. Watch the video and follow the instructions.

غ .... غ .... غ

غ .... غ .... غ

3. Watch the video and write the following words.

غَم .... پُرتِغال ....

میغ .... کَلاغ ....

4. Listen and check when you hear the /gh/ sound in the word.

۱. ☐   ۲. ☐   ۳. ☐   ۴. ☐   ۵. ☐

5. Circle the letter غ in the following text. Report to your instructor how many غ you identified in the text.

براساس نظریه متخصصین تغذیه، حواس‌پرتی و بی‌توجهی هنگام غذا خوردن بر عمل هضم و جذب غذا تاثیر منفی می‌گذارد.

تغذیه صحیح قدرت یادگیری افراد به خصوص کودکان را بالا می‌برد. همینطور نخوردن صبحانه اثرات منفی در یادگیری افراد دارد. ناشتا بودن ظرف مدت کوتاهی گلوکز خون را در سطح ثابت نگه می‌دارد و به عملکرد طبیعی مغز لطمه وارد می‌کند.

اگر مدت زمان نخوردن صبحانه طولانی شود مغز قادر به انجام فعالیت طبیعی نیست و یادگیری مختل می‌شود. با بالا رفتن قند خون استیل کولین ساخته می‌شود که در تقویت حافظه نقش اساسی دارد.

6. Listen and write the words you hear.

۱. ....
۲. ....
۳. ....
۴. ....
۵. ....

Part 2: zâ /z/ ‾‾ظ‾‾

| ظن | نَظم | حافظ |

1. Listen to the audio file for ظ zâ.

The letter *zaa* represents the fourth letter you have learned that is pronounced ز ! Like the letters ذ and ض , the letter ظ is used in words of Arabic origin. Most Persian words you learn will use ز , but when you come across words spelled with one of the other letters, you must memorize their proper spelling.

2. Watch the video and follow the instructions.

ظ ....

3. Watch the video and write the following words.

ظاهِر .... ظُهر ....

نَظَر .... خُداحافِظ ....

4. Listen and write the words you hear. Use ظ when you hear /z/ sound.

۱.   ۲.   ۳.   ۴.   ۵.

5. Read aloud the following words with your partner.

۱. اِظهارات   ۲. تَظاهُر   ۳. مَظلوم   ۴. ظُهر   ۵. مَظنون

6. Circle the letter ظ in the following text. Report to your instructor how many ظ you identified in the text.

کرمانشاه ـ خبرنگار اطلاعات: یک میلیارد و ۵۰۰ میلیون ریال اعتبار برای مطالعه سه سد در شهرستان گیلانغرب اختصاص یافت.
علیرضا نظری معاون فرماندار گیلانغرب با اظهار مطلب بالا، افزود: دو سد مخزنی و زاگرس شهرستان گیلانغرب در مرحله بهره‌برداری و دایک و دریاچه

سراب نیز آخرین مراحل تکمیل را می‌گذراند و این سدها در مناطق ویژه نان، هفت چشمه جهانشاه و باسکله در انبار این شهرستان ساخته خواهد شد.
وی گفت: طرح مطالعاتی سد مخزنی کل کش پایان یافته است و بزودی ساخت این سد شروع می‌شود.
ابراهیم دارایی مدیر اداره جهاد کشاورزی گیلانغرب نیز گفت: با برنامه‌ریزی‌های صورت گرفته تا پایان امسال شهرستان گیلانغرب موفق به تولید و تأمین سبزی مورد نیاز استان کرمانشاه خواهد شد.
وی افزود: با توجه به نزولات خوب و نگاه ویژه دولت به بخش کشاورزی در حال حاضر وضع تولید بهبود پیدا کرده و کشورمان از نظر تولید گندم رتبه دوازدهم و از نظر رشد تولید گندم رتبه سوم دنیا را در اختیار دارد.
مدیر اداره جهاد کشاورزی گیلانغرب اظهار داشت: ۷۱۵۰ کیلوگرم سموم برای مبارزه با زنگ‌زدگی مزارع گندم شهرستان گیلانغرب بین کشاورزان توزیع شده است.

روزنامه اطلاعات
خرداد ۱۳۸۹

PERSIAN OF IRAN TODAY

Vocabulary 1 — واژگان ۱

1. Listen to and learn these words. The spoken variations have been included in parentheses.

English	Example	Persian
I eat food. (never use khordan by itself)	من در رستوران غذا می‌خورم. (من تو این رستوران غذا می‌خورم.)	۱. غَذا می‌خورم
morning / breakfast	من صبح کار می‌کنم. من صبحانه نمی‌خورم.	۲. صُبح/ صُبحانه
good morning.	صبح به خیر مادر!	۳. صُبح به خِیر
greeting for noon	ظهرتون به خیر!	۴. ظهر به خیر
good afternoon.	عصر شما به خیر!	۵. عصر به خیر
good night. (when you are going to bed at night)	شب به خیر دخترم!	۶. شَب به خِیر
how many?	چند رستوران در این خیابان است؟ (چند رستوران تو این خیابون هست؟)	۷. چَند؟
what time? when?	ساعت چند ناهار می‌خورید؟ کی ناهار می‌خورید؟	۸. ساعت چند؟/ کِی
two o'clock	ساعت دو ناهار می‌خوریم.	۹. ساعتِ دو
one o'clock	ساعت یک در خانه هستی؟ (... تو خونه هستی؟)	۱۰. ساعتِ یک
what?	ناهار چه چیزی می‌خورید؟ (ناهار چی می‌خورین؟)	۱۱. چه/ چه چیزی/چی؟
occupation	(شغل پدر شما چیه؟)	۱۲. شغل
I was	من دیروز ناراحت بودم، اما امروز خوشحالم.	۱۳. بودم
I was not	ساعت دو گرسنه بودم، اما الان گرسنه نیستم.	۱۴. نبودم
now	الان گرسنه نیستم.	۱۵. الان

2. Listen to the audio file again. Based on what you hear, write the vowels on the example sentences. Now listen to the next audio file. Write the sentences you hear and translate them to English.

واژگان ۲ — Vocabulary 2

Numbers

3. Listen to the audio file. Translate the sample sentences into English. Then follow the pattern for numbers 20 through 30 to write the numbers 31 through 40. Read them aloud and write a sentence for each number.

twenty one	بیست و یک صندلی در این کلاس است.(بیست و یه صندلی تو این کلاس هست.)		بیست و یک
twenty two	آن مرد تبریزی بیست و دو بچه دارد.(اون مرد تبریزی بیست و دو تا بچه داره.)		بیست و دو
twenty three	این دختر جوان بیست و سه سال دارد. (این دختر جوون بیست و سه سالشه.)		بیست و سه
twenty four	بیست و چهار مرد جوان در کلاس بودند. (بیست و چهار مرد جوون تو کلاس بودن.)		بیست و چهار
twenty five	من و بیست و پنج نفر از دوستانم به ترکیه می‌رویم. (من و بیست و پنج تا از دوستام می‌ریم ترکیه.)		بیست و پنج
twenty six	من بیست و شش دانشجو دارم. (من بیست و شیش تا دانشجو دارم.)		بیست و شش
twenty seven	بیست و هفت مداد دارم. (... تا مداد دارم.)		بیست و هفت
twenty eight	بیست و هشت کتاب فارسی آنجاست. (... تا کتاب فارسی اونجاست.)		بیست و هشت
twenty nine	این بیست و نه دانش آموز یک معلّم دارند. (.... تا دانش‌آموز یه معلّم دارن.)		بیست و نه
thirty	من سی سال دارم. (من سی سالمه.)		سی

4. Listen to the audio file again. Based on what you hear, write the vowels on the example sentences. Now listen to the next audio file. Write the sentences you hear and translate them to English.

چرا

Read the following questions and answers:

ناهار می‌خورید؟ . بله
ناهار می‌خورید؟ -نه
ناهار نمی‌خورید؟ -چرا، می‌خورم.

5. Can you guess what چرا means in the third sentence? As you know, we use "بله" to mean "yes" in the affirmative. How do we respond "yes" to a negative question? Explain the rule.

....

....

6. Write possible questions for the following answers.

۱. ....؟ چرا، این‌جا زندگی می‌کنم.

۲. ....؟ چرا، دوست دارم.

۳. ....؟ چرا، خسته‌ام.

۴. ....؟ چرا، دارم.

Memorize these two phrases for future use!

~ From now on, when somone sneezes in class, you should say the following expression, which literately means, "may it be healthy": عافیت باشه /âfiyat bâshe/.

~ The person who has sneezed can answer with the following sentence which literary means "may you be healthy": سلامت باشید /salâmat bâshid/.

Listening Comprehension   درک شنیدار

Watch the videos and answer the following questions in Persian. Try to answer in complete sentences whenever it is possible.

1. Whose picture did Shayli show us?
2. What did you learn about the people whose pictures Shayli showed us?
3. What was the first word that Shayli said when she picked up the phone?
4. Who called Shayli?
5. What information did she give to Shayli?
6. How does Shayli say goodbye?

7. How does Shayli feel when she arrives home from school?
8. How is the weather today?
9. Where does she decide to go?
10. What do you think she is planning to eat?
11. How does Shayli feel when she is leaving the house?

12. What does Leili say when she calls?
13. What do you think /manzel/ means in Persian?
14. What does the man say?
15. What does Leili say to apologize? How does the man answer the apology?

What time is it?

1. Listen to the audio file to find out what time it is and how you ask the time in Persian. Repeat what you hear several times so that you are ready to ask your classmates later.

 Time 1

مریم: (ببخشید، ساعت چنده؟)
رهگذر: (ساعت هشته.)

2. Listen to the audio file and find out how we tell time in Persian. The audio file includes both the written and spoken forms. Underline the differences and be prepared to discuss them in class.

 Time 2

عدد	گفتاری	نوشتاری
۹:۰۰	۱. ساعت نهه.	۱. ساعت نه است.
۹:۰۵	۲. ساعت نه و پنج دقیقه‌ست.	۲. ساعت نه و پنج دقیقه است.
۹:۱۵	۳. ساعت نه و پانزده دقیقه‌ست. ساعت نه و ربعه.	۳. ساعت نه و پانزده دقیقه است. ساعت نه و ربع است.
۹:۳۰	۴. ساعت نه و سی دقیقه‌ست. ساعت نه و نیمه.	۴. ساعت نه و سی دقیقه است. ساعت نه و نیم است.
۹:۴۵	۵. ساعت نه و چهل و پنج دقیقه‌ست. ساعت یک ربع به ده‌ه.	۵. ساعت نه و چهل و پنج دقیقه است. ساعت یک ربع به ده است.
۱۰:۰۰	۶. ساعت ده‌ه.	۶. ساعت ده است.

3. What time is it in different cities now?

```
NTP Time Zone Clock
File Help

12:30   Paris
11:30   London
06:30   New York
03:30   San Francisco
```

الان در پاریس ساعت ....، در لندن ساعت ....،
در نیویورک ساعت ....،
و در سانفرانسیسکو ساعت .... است.

149 PERSIAN OF IRAN TODAY

4. Listen to the audio file. Then, read the following sentences for yourself and find the related clocks. Underline the words you do not know and guess what they mean.

۱. ساعت دوازده است.

۲. ساعت دوازده و پنج دقیقه است.

۳. ساعت دوازده و ده دقیقه است.

۴. ساعت دوازده و پانزده دقیقه است. / ساعت دوازده و ربع است.

۵. ساعت دوازده و بیست دقیقه است.

۶. ساعت دوازده و بیست و پنج دقیقه است.

۷. ساعت دوازده و نیم است.

۸. ساعت دوازده و سی و پنج دقیقه است./ ساعت بیست و پنج دقیقه به یک است.

۹. ساعت دوازده و چهل دقیقه است./ ساعت بیست دقیقه به یک است.

۱۰. ساعت دوازده و چهل و پنج دقیقه است. / ساعت یک ربع به یک است.

۱۱. ساعت دوازده و پنجاه دقیقه است. / ساعت ده دقیقه به یک است.

۱۲. ساعت دوازده و پنجاه و پنج دقیقه است. / ساعت پنج دقیقه به یک است.

5. Read the following sentences and write the appropriate time.

مثال: ساعت هشت و چهل دقیقه است. /ساعت بیست دقیقه به نه است.   ....۸:۴۰......

۱. ساعت شش و دوازده دقیقه است.   ....

۲. ساعت شش و پانزده دقیقه است. / ساعت شش و ربع است.   ....

۳. ساعت شش و سی دقیقه است. / ساعت شش و نیم است.   ....

۴. ساعت شش و چهل و پنج دقیقه است. / ساعت یک ربع به هفت است.   ....

۵. ساعت هفت است.   ....

6. In the following text, there are several words that you do not know. Underline them and guess what they mean. Be prepared to discuss how you arrived at your answer in class.

این ساعت من است. (این ساعت منه.)

من ساعت بزرگ دوست دارم. این ساعت من است. ساعتم سه عقربه دارد: عقربه‌ی ساعت شمار، عقربه‌ی دقیقه شمار، و عقربه‌ی ثانیه شمار

Writing exercise نوشتن

Use the vocabulary you have learned to write a conversation. Your conversation should have a setting (a restaurant, a class) and a short narrative. Write at least 20 sentences for your conversation.

Speaking Activities حرف زدن

Homework:

Review the vocabulary and grammar for this lesson and think about how you would ask (and answer) the following questions. Practice them aloud until you can ask them comfortably.

At what time do you eat breakfast?
Where do you eat dinner?
How many brothers do you have? How many sisters?
When do you go to class?
How many chairs are in your house?

In class:

1. Watch Video 9 with your instructor and learn a few new greetings. Try using them with several classmates, and then ask the questions above. Remember what your classmates say so that you can report back to the rest of the class later.

2. First greet your partner using one of the new greetings you've learned. Then in spoken Persian, take turns practicing asking each other: a) where you were at different times yesterday (دیروز) and today (اِمروز), and b) where you will go at different times today and tomorrow (فردا).

Language Games

1. The instructor will write a sentence on the board. The group with the most questions related to that sentence will be the winner.
مثال : در تهران در یک رستوران ایرانی غذای مکزیکی می‌خورم.

2. The instructor will write 20 words on the board and then erase them. Groups of three have 45 seconds to write down as many words as they remember on a piece of paper. Words with incorrect spellings will not be counted.

3. The class is divided into groups of 3 to 5. The students will tell their team how they felt yesterday (دیروز) and how they feel now.

دیروز خسته بودم، اما امروز خسته نیستم. امروز مریض هستم.

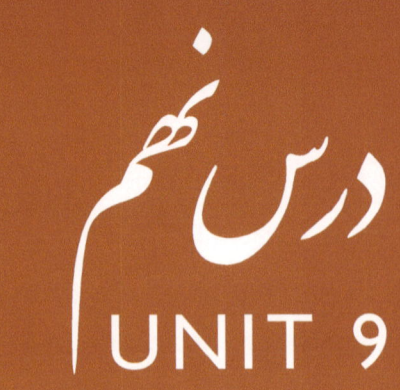

درس نهم
UNIT 9

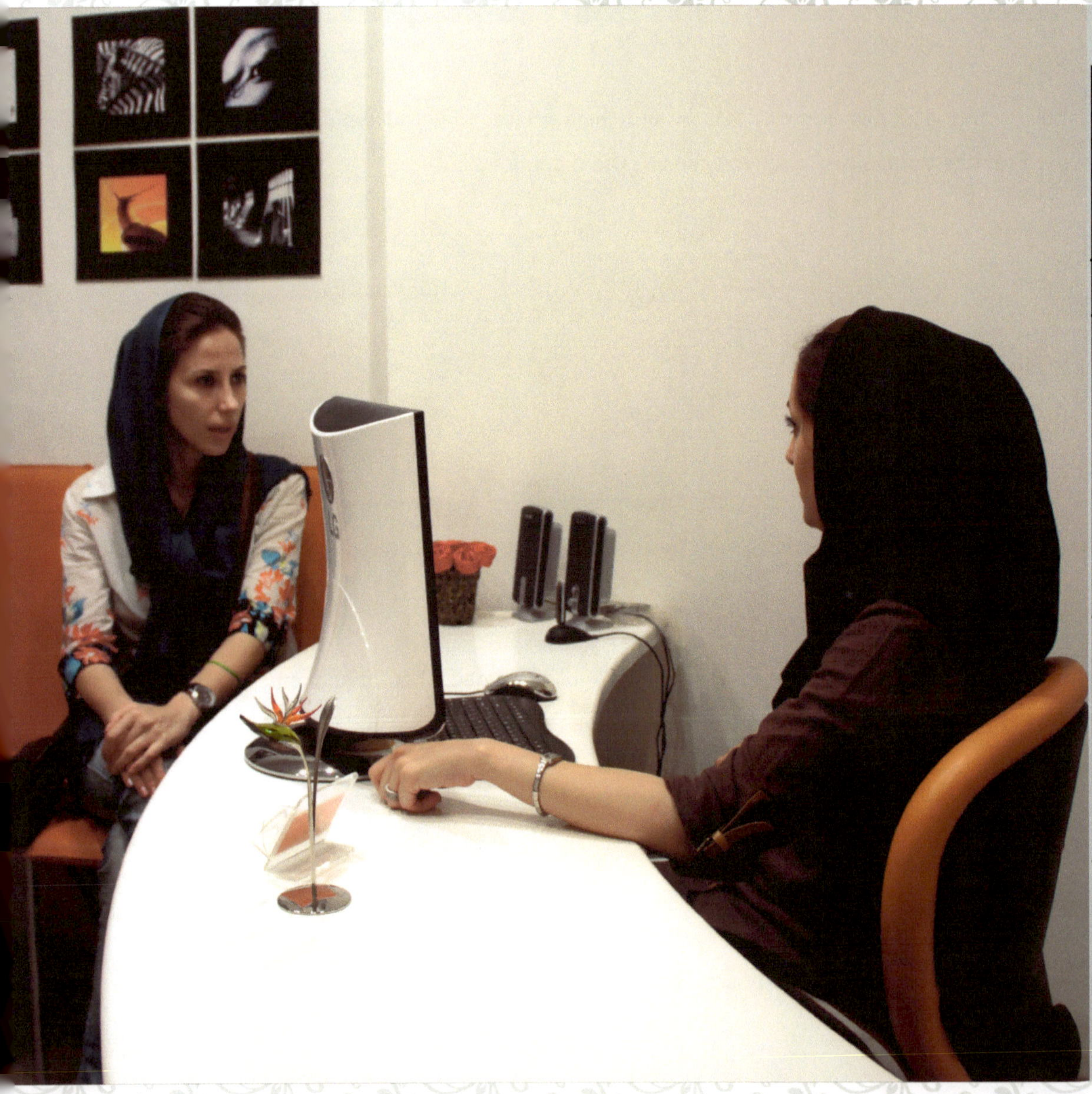

ص	آ
ض	ب
ط	پ
ظ	ت
ع	ث
غ	ج
ف	چ
ق	ح
ک	خ
گ	د
ل	ذ
م	ر
ن	ز
و	ژ
ه	س
ی	ش

What do you do?/ What is your job?

شما چه‌کار می‌کنید؟ / شما چه کاره هستید؟/ شغل شما چیه؟

Cultural Note — یادداشت فرهنگی

بِفَرمایید

بفرمایید is one of the most important and most commonly used expressions in Persian. Its meaning shifts and changes according to the context in which it is used; however, in general it is a polite way of asking someone to do something. The word can be coupled with commands so that the speaker's request is clear. You could say, for example, بفرمایید بشینید to mean "please sit down" or "go ahead and sit."

The word is used by itself, and the speaker's request or command is clarified by hand gestures and/or the context. For example, when a visitor arrives, you might invite him or her in by saying بفرمایید and signaling inside. Similarly, you might give up your seat at a party and encourage someone else to sit in your spot by saying بفرمایید and pointing at the seat. This word is also used to encourage someone to do something first. So if two people are entering a building at the same time, one person will allow the other to enter first by بِفَرمایید.

Or if two people start talking at the same time, one person will allow the other to begin by saying بفرمایید. In Iranian culture, it is polite to allow the other person to do things first, so sometimes two people will exchange بفرمایید, both encouraging the other to go ahead and speak, enter, eat, etc. first.

Just as hand gestures are often important, so too is one's tone of voice. Using a warm, encouraging tone lets your listeners know that you want them to do something, while using a firm tone is a way of exerting your control and requesting that they not do something. بفرمایید is part of a system of politeness in Persian called تعارف, about which you will learn more as you continue your study of Persian!

You will often hear مُزاحِمِتون نمی شم in response to بفرمایید as a way of saying "I don't want to bother you..."

In class, work in groups of three and prepare a skit that only uses the word بفرمایید. Remember to use lots of hand gestures so that your intentions are clear!

Short Conversations گفتگوهای کوتاه

In class, listen to the audio files, repeat what you hear and try to fill in the blanks. At home repeat what you hear several times and try to follow the rhythm. Write at least two sentences in Persian about each conversation you hear. During the next class time, you will work with a classmate to create a scenario that uses these expressions.

- سلام، شما در این .... زندگی می‌کنید؟
- بله.
- چه .... هستید؟
- .... عمران هستم.
- این‌جا .... دوست دارید؟
- بله، .... زیاد.

1. ....
2. ....

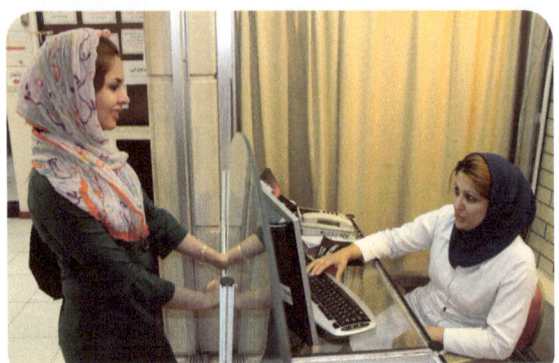

- سلام، شما این‌جا .... ؟
- بله.
- .... کار می‌کنید؟ .... هستید؟
- نه، .... هستم.
- دانشجوی چی؟
- دانشجوی .... هستم.

1. ....
2. ....

- سلام، شما .... چیه؟
- من .... هستم.
- اوه! شما خیلی جوون .... !

1. ....
2. ....

In this unit, you will learn about certain grammatical markers that are used in Persian.

تنوین	همزه	سکون

Part 1: *tanvin* /t/ ــً

لطفاً

1. Listen to the audio file for تنوین *tanvin*.

The word tanvin refers to the *an* sound that is found at the end of certain adverbs. The /an/ sound is represented in writing by the doubling of the zebar vowel symbol above *alef*.

2. Writing tanvin: Watch the video and follow the instructions.

اً ....

3. Watch the video and write the following words.

حَتماً .... کامِلاً ....

4. Listen and check when the word needs *tanvin* at the end.

☐ ۱. ☐ ۲. ☐ ۳. ☐ ۴. ☐ ۵. ☐ ۶. ☐ ۷. ☐ ۸.

5. Circle اً in the following texts. Report to your instructor how many اً you identified in the text.

آیا واقعاً افراد مبتلا به دیابت می‌توانند ورزش کنند و اصولاً چه نکاتی را باید هنگام ورزش رعایت کنند؟

لطفاً کتابها رو از روی میز بردار و همه رو ببر کتابخونه. من دارم میرم دانشگاه و حتماً تا ساعت نه برمیگردم که بریم سینما.

6. Listen and write the words you hear.

۱. .... ۲. .... ۳. .... ۴. .... ۵. ....

| مطمئن | سؤال |

Part 2: hamze ـئـ ـؤ أ

1. Listen to the audio file for *hamze*.

Hamze is a marker representing the same sound as the letter *eyn*. It doesn't have an independent alphabetic form, but instead sits on top of other consonants, specifically *alef*, *vâv*, and *ye*. *Hamze* only occurs in words of foreign origin.

2. Watch the video and follow the instructions.

ؤ .... أ ....

3. Watch the video and write the following words.

تئاتر ....

سئول ....

مسئول ....

جامائیکا ....

4. Circle *hamze* in the following texts. Report to your instructor how many *hamze* you identified in the text.

روزنامه اطلاعات
خرداد ۱۳۸۹

امشب میریم تئاتر بعد هم می‌ریم خونه‌ی سمانه. خونه‌شون تو خیابون سئوله.

Part 3: *sokun* ◌ْ

سَرْد

1. Listen to the audio file for ◌ْ *sokun*.

This symbol is a pronunciation marker that indicates the absence of a vowel. So far, you have learned to use *zir*, *pish*, and *zebar* over consonants to indicate vowels, and consonants not followed by a vowel have been left "blank." If you want to clarify that there is no vowel between two consonants, you use a *sokun*.

Like the short vowel symbols, the *sokun* is rarely used in unvocalized or partially vocalized texts. When it is written, it appears as a small open circle above a letter not followed by a vowel. In writing *sokun*, make sure to draw a closed circle and not a *pish* or a dot.

2. Watch the video and follow the instructions.

…………………………………ْ◌

3. Circle *sokun* in the following texts. Report to your instructor how many *sokun* you identified in the text.

بِسْمِ ٱللَّهِ ٱلرَّحْمَٰنِ ٱلرَّحِيمِ
ٱلْحَمْدُ لِلَّهِ رَبِّ ٱلْعَٰلَمِينَ ۝ ٱلرَّحْمَٰنِ
ٱلرَّحِيمِ ۝ مَٰلِكِ يَوْمِ ٱلدِّينِ ۝ إِيَّاكَ
نَعْبُدُ وَإِيَّاكَ نَسْتَعِينُ ۝ ٱهْدِنَا
ٱلصِّرَٰطَ ٱلْمُسْتَقِيمَ ۝ صِرَٰطَ ٱلَّذِينَ
أَنْعَمْتَ عَلَيْهِمْ غَيْرِ ٱلْمَغْضُوبِ عَلَيْهِمْ
وَلَا ٱلضَّآلِّينَ ۝

4. Read the following words aloud with your partner.

۱. تَقریباً	۲. رأس	۳. واقِعاً	۴. تِئاتر
۵. اَوَّلاً	۶. تِئوری	۷. حَتماً	۸. مُتأسِّفانه
۹. حَتمَن	۱۰. مُؤَسِّسه	۱۱. غالِباً	۱۲. سُؤال
۱۳. اُصولاً	۱۴. پَنگوئَن	۱۵. مَعمولاً	۱۶. کاکائو
۱۷. بَعداً	۱۸. مَنشأ	۱۹. قَبلاً	۲۰. مأمور
۲۱. توأم	۲۲. شأن	۲۳. رأی	۲۴. مأوا

واژگان Vocabulary 1

1. Listen to and learn these words. The spoken variations have been included in parentheses.

English	Example (spoken)	Persian
What are you doing?	شما صبح چه کار می کنید؟ (شما صبح چه کار می‌کنین؟)	۱. چه کار می‌کُنید؟
what do you do?	شما چه کاره هستید؟ (شما چه کاره هستین؟)	۲. چه کاره هستید؟
what is your job?	شغل شما چیست، آقا؟ (شغل شما چیه آقا؟)	۳. شُغلِ شما چیست؟ (شغل شما چیه؟)
what does he do? What do they do?	پدر شما چه کاره هستند؟ (پدر شما چه کاره هستن؟)	۴. چه کاره هستند؟
how are you?	سلام، حال شما چه طوره؟	۵. حال شما چه طور است؟ (... چه طوره؟)
question	من یک سوال دارم. (من یه سوال دارم.)	۶. سوال
answer	جواب این سوال آسان است. (جواب این سوال آسونه.)	۷. جواب
doctor	پدر من دکتر است. (پدر من دکتره.)	۸. دُکتُر
engineer	پدر او مهندس است. (پدر اون مهندسه.)	۹. مُهَندِس
nurse	مادر آنها پرستار است. (مادر اونا پرستاره.)	۱۰. پَرستار
teacher	مادر شما معلم است؟ (مادر شما معلّمه؟)	۱۱. مُعَلِّم
house wife	مادرتان خانه‌دار است؟ (مادرتون خانه‌داره؟)	۱۲. خانه‌دار
student (non-university)	این معلم فارسی پانزده دانش آموز دارد. (این معلم فارسی پانزده تا دانش آموز داره.)	۱۳. دانِش‌آموز/ شاگِرد
lawyer	خواهرم وکیل است. (خواهرم وکیله.)	۱۴. وَکیل
journalist	برادر تو روزنامه نگار است؟ (برادر تو روزنامه نگاره؟)	۱۵. روزنامه‌نگار/ خبرنگار
house wife	مادر من خانه دار است. (مادر من خونه‌داره.)	۱۶. خانه‌دار
Quantifier	چند تا مداد روی میز است؟ (چند تا مداد روی میزه؟)	۱۷. تا
Quantifier for person	چند نفر در کلاس هستند؟ (چند نفر تو کلاس هستن؟)	۱۸. نَفَر
because	من امروز دو تا ساندویچ بزرگ خوردم چون خیلی گرسنه بودم.	۱۹. چون

Review the various prepositions below. Examine the following images, and write the preposition that best describes the dot's relationship to the box.

واژگان — Vocabulary 2

2. Listen to and learn these words. The spoken variations have been included in parentheses. **Note that we add *ezâfe* to prepositions 17–24 when they are preceded by a noun or pronoun.**

English	Example	Persian
in	خانه‌ی ما در تهران است. (خونه‌ی ما تو تهرونه.)	۲۰. دَر
on	مدادم روی دفتر بود. الان نیست. کجاست؟	۲۱. رو، روی
under	خودکار من زیر کتاب شما است؟ (خودکار من زیر کتاب شماست.)	۱۸. زیر
close	خانه‌ات نزدیک دانشگاه است؟ (خونه‌ات نزدیک دانشگاه ست.)	۱۹. نَزدیک
beside	خانه‌ی ما کنار خانه‌ی آنها است. (خونه‌ی ما کنار خونه‌ی اوناست.)	۲۰. کنار
in front of	کتابخانه جلوی دانشگاه است. (کتابخونه جلوی دانشگاهه.)	۲۱. جلو
over/above	خانه‌ی آنها بالای خانه‌ی شماست. (خونه‌ی اونا بالای خونه‌ی شماست.)	۲۲. بالا
behind	ساعتم پشت کیف شما نیست؟	۲۳. پُشت
between	یک صندلی بین دو دیوار است. (........ دیواره.)	۲۴. بین

3. Listen to the audio file again. Based on what you hear, write the vowel on the example sentences. Now listen to the next audio file. Write the sentences you hear and translate them to English.

Memorize this sentence!

"book" به فارسی چی می‌شه؟

What is "book" in Persian?

Now ask your classmate the meanings of five words in Persian.

Listening Comprehension — درک شنیدار

Watch the videos and answer the following questions.

1. What did you learn about the people in this video?
2. Answer Raha's questions.
3. When does this conversation take place? At what time of day?
4. What are Shayli's plans for tonight? Where will she go? When? With whom?
5. Guess how Shayli says "it was fun."

۶- خودکار شایلی کجاست؟

7. Shyli has lots of questions for Sadaf. What does she want to know and what does she find out?

Grammar Note — یادداشت دستوری

Possessive Pronouns

The possessive pronouns (mine, yours, his, hers, etc.) are made by putting مالِ /mâle/ before the personal pronouns. Complete the following chart!

این کتاب مال من نیست.	This book is not mine	مال من	من
....	That ice cream is yours.	....	شما/تو
....	This book is hers.	....	ایشان/او (ایشون/ اون)
....	That tea is ours.	....	ما
....	This is not yours.	....	شما
....	Is this theirs?	....	آنها (اونا)

Now, guess the meaning of the following sentences.

۱.	۱. این کتاب مال کیه؟
۲.	۲. این بستنی مال شماست؟
۳.	۳. (اون نون مال کیه؟ مال شما نیست؟)

Counting (continued)

In Lesson Five, you learned that singular nouns always follow numbers in Persian. So instead of saying "five men," like you would in English, we say پنج مرد, using the singular (مرد). In the next lesson, you'll learn more about plurals in Persian. However, as you master the plural don't forget that after numbers, always use the singular!

Asking "how many?"

In order to ask "how many" of something in Persian, we use چند تا. You will recognize چند from the previous lesson when you learned to ask 'what time' (ساعت چند). This word is the question word for numbers in Persian, meaning usually when the answer is a number we use چند as the question word. For now, in order to ask "how many" of a specific person or thing, we follow چند with the word تا, which has no equivalent in English but is a counting word in Persian. A different word is used for asking how many people in general: نفر.

چند تا کتاب دارید؟	How many books do you have?
چند تا دانشجو در این کلاس هست؟	How many students are in this class?
چند تا دفتر در کیفتان است؟	How many notebooks are in your bag?
چند نفر در آستین زندگی می‌کنند؟	How many people live in Austin?

What do you notice about the nouns that follow چند تا?
....

Like numbers چند is always followed by a singular noun. However, look at the verb in the two sentences with چند تا. How are the verbs conjugated? For which person?...

*When you ask the question or make a statement چند نفر, you always conjugate the verb for آنها. Can you find the sentence from the examples above that uses this construction? ....

*When you ask the question چند تا and you are asking about inanimate objects, you conjugate the verb for the third person-singular. Can you find the example? ....

*When you ask the question چند تا and you are asking about people, then you can either conjugate the verb in the third-person singular or plural. Can you find the example? ....

Note: Sometimes تا is excluded from the question چند تا. At the same time, by itself چند can mean "several" or "a few." In this case it is still followed by *singular* nouns! Intonation, then, becomes important to distinguishing between a statement of "several" and a question of "how many." Practice reading the following examples, paying close attention to the intonation of a question.

چند وکیل؟	How many lawyers?
چند وکیل	several lawyers
چند شب؟	How many nights?
چند شب	several nights

Answering "how many?"
In order to answer this question using a full statement, you simply replace چند with the appropriate number, making sure to still use the singular noun. The use of تا is optional as long as you list the item that is being counted. Look at the following answers to the questions above.

پنج تا کتاب دارم.	I have five books.
پانزده نفر در این کلاس هستند.	There are fifteen people in this class.
سه دفتر در کیفم است.	There are three notebooks in my bag.
۸۰۰٬۰۰۰ نفر در آستین زندگی می‌کنند.	800,000 people live in Austin.

The use of تا in sentences like these is primarily a feature of the spoken language. In writing, تا is usually omitted.

Note: In the course of a conversation, it is far more common to answer the question "how many?" with just the number, rather than a whole sentence. However, in Persian we can never answer the questions چند تا or چند نفر with a number alone. Instead, we say the number and the item being counted or the number and تا or نفر. The one exception to this rule is the number one (یک). We **NEVER** say or write یک تا in this context; instead we simply say or write یکی.

Examine questions and corresponding answers:

چند تا کتاب دارین؟	پنج تا
چند نفر تو این کلاس هستن؟	پونزده شاگرد
چند تا دفتر تو کیفتون هست؟	یکی
چند نفر تو آستین زندگی می‌کنن؟	۸۰۰٬۰۰۰ نفر

Grammar Practice: Answer the following questions with complete sentences. The questions are in written form. How would you answer them differently in conversation?

۱. چند تا مداد روی میز است؟ ....

۲. چند نفر این‌جا هستند؟ ....

۳. چند تا کتاب در کیف داری؟ ....

۴. چند نفر در خانه‌اتان زندگی می‌کنند؟ ....

Review: Counting in Persian is relatively simple. However, it is confusing at first because there are new terms and concepts that do not exist in English. Take some time and explain the following Persian terms in English, making sure you account for the various meanings and usages of each term.

چند ....

تا ....

نفر ....

یکی ....

One more thing about the verb "to be."

In spoken Persian, if you want to indicate that "there is" something or "there are" some things, it is **common** to use هست. Look at the following examples.

There is a big door in front of the student.	(یه در بزرگ جلوی دانش‌آموز هست.)
There are six questions.	(شیش تا سوال هست.)
There are several books under the table.	(چند تا کتاب زیر میز هست.)

Note: This use of هست is usually only found in the spoken language.

Fill in the blanks using هست or ه/ـه . Be prepared to explain your answers in class. All of the sentences below are in spoken form. In some cases both options are correct.

امروز هوا خیلی گرم ....
چند خونه توی این خیابون ....
چند تا اتاق توی اون خونه .... ؟
دوست برادرم مریض ....
اصفهان شهر زیبایی ....
یه کیف بزرگ روی میز ....
اون کیف روی میز مال کی .... ؟
اون فیلم خیلی خوب ....
کی الان خونه .... ؟

نوشتن Writing Exercise

Take a picture of your room and print it out (or find a picture of a room on the Web). Use the words you have learned to describe the picture. The following questions may help you develop your paragraph.

What is this picture (عکس)?
What is my name? What do I do? Where do I live? Do I have a room? Do I share it with somebody? Is the room big? What do I have in the room? Where are things are located? Is the room clean (تمیز)?

Speaking Activities

In Class:

Look at the pictures below and use the new vocabulary to describe them. For example:

مداد روی کتاب است.
(دو تا صندلی کنار میز هست.)

For Homework:

Review the vocabulary and grammar and think about how you would ask (and answer) these questions. Practice aloud so you are ready to ask your classmates.

~ What does your father do? What time does he go to work?
~ Is your mother a doctor? What's your mother's job?
~ Is your brother a lawyer? Is your sister an engineer?
~ What do you do? Do you like your work?
~ Is your mother a nurse?
~ What is in front of your house?
~ Why do you like Persian?
~ Now how many people are in our class?
~ Are your brothers or sisters students?
~ Where were you yesterday at noon?

Language Game

Hoarders

Work in small groups. Make sure your books are closed, and then describe an imaginary room in a minute and forty-five seconds. Your instructor will draw the room as you describe it. However, he or she may refuse to draw sentences that are incorrect. After each group has finished, the items in each picture will be counted, and the group with the most items in its room wins!

درس دهم

UNIT 10

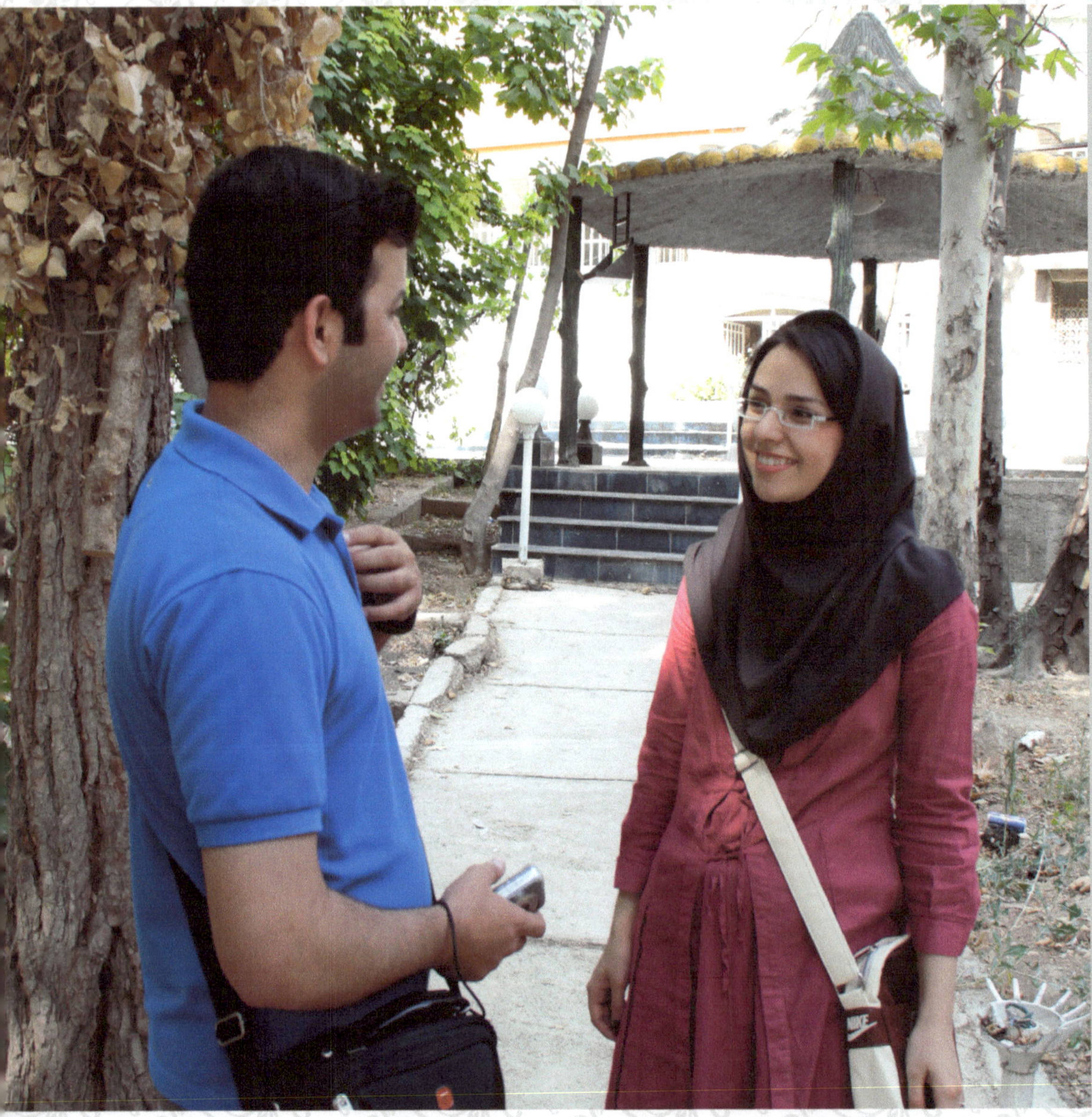

ص	آ
ض	ب
ط	پ
ظ	ت
ع	ث
غ	ج
ف	چ
ق	ح
ک	خ
گ	د
ل	ذ
م	ر
ن	ز
و	ژ
ه	س
ی	ش

What is your major? رشته‌تون چیه؟

Cultural Note · یادداشت فرهنگی

نظام آموزشی در ایران

Educational System in Iran

Education in Iran is an extensive system that can be divided into two parts: primary/secondary education and higher education. While the Ministry of Education oversees the former, the latter is supervised y theMinistry of Science, Research, and Technology. All levels of education are free in Iran; however, private institutions exist both at the university level and the primary/secondary level.

According to the Iranian constitution, all Iranians must achieve at least a primary education. In Iran, there is an optional year-long pre-elementary course that students begin at age 5 or 6. Elementary school or دبستان begins the following year and lasts five years. At the end of that period, students must pass nationally administered exams to continue to the next level. Middle school, which is called راهنمایی, or guidance, is a three-year program that prepares students for high school, or دبیرستان. Secondary education is not required in Iran. However, students who decide to continue can choose two tracks during their three years in دبیرستان: an academic/theoretical track that prepares them for higher education, or a vocational track to prepare them for the work force. At the end of دبیرستان students receive a دیپلم متوسطه. Primary and secondary education in Iran is divided according to gender, and girls and boys attend different institutions.

Students who wish to continue on to higher education must pass a national entrance exam called کُنکور. Students usually spend an entire year preparing for this exam, and admission into universities is contingent upon the score they achieve. There are separate exams for admission into public and private institutions, and admission into public institutions tends to be more competitive because tuition is free. Fields in science and technology and professional programs (like medicine and dentistry) are especially competitive.

Unlike primary and secondary education, most institutions of higher learning are open to both men and women. However, classrooms are divided by gender and men sit on one side and women on the other. Academic years are divided into semesters, and at the end of approximately four years, students receive a لیسانس / کارشناسی, which is equivalent to a bachelor's degree in the United States. فوق لیسانس / کارشناسی ارشد, which is equivalent to a master's degree, can usually be completed in two years (beyond کارشناسی). A دکترا (or پی اچ دی, as it is sometimes called in conversation) is the highest degree attainable in most fields.

PERSIAN OF IRAN TODAY

Short Conversations گفت‌وگوهای کوتاه

In class, listen to the audio files, repeat what you hear and try to fill in the blanks. At home repeat what you hear several times and try to follow the rhythm. Write at least two sentences in Persian about each conversation you hear. During the next class time, you will work with a classmate to create a scenario that uses these expressions.

_ دانشجوی این .... هستین؟

_ بله.

_ .... چیه؟

_ تاریخ ....

_ من هم ....

_ سال چندم .... ؟

_ سال اول

_ شما .... هستین؟

_ من .... سوم هستم.

_ سلام ، دخترتون .... ؟

_ بله.

_ .... هستن؟

_ بله، دخترم .... سال سوم.

_ پسرمن .... دانشجوئه. دانشجوی مهندسی.

۱. ....

۲. ....

How do you say "major in Persian? Add this word to the list of vocabulary in this unit.

۱. ....

۲. ....

جدول الفبا   گوش کنید و تکرار کنید.

الف	بِ	پِ	تِ	ثِ	جیم	چِ	حِ	خِ	دال	ذال	رِ	زِ	ژِ	سین	شین
آ	ب	پ	ت	ث	ج	چ	ح	خ	د	ذ	ر	ز	ژ	س	ش
صاد	ضاد	طا	ظا	عین	غین	فِ	قاف	کاف	گاف	لام	میم	نون	واو	هِ	ی
ص	ض	ط	ظ	ع	غ	ف	ق	ک	گ	ل	م	ن	و	ه	ی

واژگان ۱: واژگان کلاس   Vocabulary 1

1. Listen to and learn these words. The spoken variations have been included in parentheses.

		English
۱. دَرس	این درس سخت است. (.... سخته.)	lesson
۲. تَمرین	این تمرین کتاب آسان است. (..آسون..)	exercise
۳. گوش کُنید (گوش کنین)	به این درس گوش کنید. (.... گوش کنین.)	listen, listen to
۴. حَرف بِزَنید (حرف بزنین)	با دوستم فارسی حرف بزنید. (.... حرف بزنین.)	speak
۵. بِنویسید (بنویسین)	این را در دفتر بنویسید. (اینو تو دفتر بنویسین.)	write
۶. بِخوانید (بخونین)	این کتاب فارسی را بخوانید. (...... فارسی رو بخونین.)	read
۷. تِکرار کُنید (تکرار کنین)	این تمرین را در خانه تکرار کنید. (این تمرین رو تو خونه تکرار کنین.)	repeat
۸. حَدس بِزَنید (حدس بزنین)	جواب این سوال را حدس بزنید. (جواب این سوال رو حدس بزنین.)	guess
۹. باز کُنید (باز کنین)	کتابتان را باز کنید. (کتابتون رو باز کنین.)	open
۱۰. بِبَندید (ببندین)	کتابتان را ببندید. (کتابتون رو ببندین.)	close
۱۱. کَلَمه، واژه	این کلمه را در دفترتان بنویسید. (... رو تو دفترتون بنویسین.)	word
۱۲. جُمله	این جمله را بخوانید. (.... رو بخونین.)	sentence
۱۳. عِبارت	این عبارت را تکرار کنید. (..... رو تکرار کنین.)	term, phrase
۱۴. آسان (آسون)	این ورزش آسان است. (این ورزش آسونه.)	easy
۱۵. سَخت	این درس سخت است. (.... سخته.)	hard, difficult
۱۶. رِشته	رشته‌ی شما در دانشگاه چیست؟ (رشته‌ی شما تو دانشگاه چیه؟)	major

2. Listen to the audio file again. Based on what you hear, write the vowels on the example sentences. Now listen to the next audio file. Write the sentences you hear and translate them to English.

PERSIAN OF IRAN TODAY

واژگان Vocabulary 2

کِشوَر	مِلّیَت
ایران	ایرانی
آلمان	آلمانی
آمریکا	آمریکایی
امارات	اماراتی
افغانستان	افغان

3. Look at the following list of countries and corresponding nationalities. Read them aloud with a partner and then try to identify patterns for forming nationalities based on country names. Do they all follow the rule? Circle the examples that don't follow the rule. Listen to the audio file. In addition to the words from the chart, you will hear several other countries and nationalities. Write them down and add them to your vocabulary list.

کِشوَر، مِلّیَت		4. Fill in the left column with the corresponding nationalities.
افغانستان، افغان: اهل افغانستان	آنها اهل افغانستان هستند. (اونا اهل افغانستان هستن)	
تاجیکستان، تاجیک: اهل تاجیکستان	شما اهل تاجیکستان هستید؟ (شما اهل تاجیکستان هستین؟)	
پاکستان، پاکستانی: اهل پاکستان	تو اهل پاکستان هستی؟	
عراق، عراقی: اهل عراق	عراق کنار ایران است. (عراق کنار ایران ایرانه.)	
ترکیه، اهل ترکیه	ما اهل ترکیه هستیم. Note: we should not use Tork	
ارمنستان، اهل ارمنستان	من اهل ارمنستان هستم. Note: we should not use Armani	
ترکمنستان، اهل ترکمنستان	دوستم در ترکمنستان زندگی می‌کند. (دوستم در ترکمنستان زندگی می‌کنه.)	
روسیه، روس: اهل روسیه	روسیه بالای ترکمنستان است. (روسیه بالای ترکمنستانه.)	
هند، هندی: اهل هند	او هندی است. (اون هندیه.)	
چین، چینی: اهل چین	چین بزرگ است. (چین بزرگه.)	
ژاپن، ژاپنی: اهل ژاپن	برادرم در ژاپن زندگی می‌کند. (برادرم در ژاپن زندگی می‌کنه.)	
انگلیس، انگلیسی: اهل انگلیس	او اهل انگلیس است؟ (اون اهل انگلیسه.)	

5. Add four countries that you would like to visit. Look them up on Wikipedia by searching for the country in English and then selecting Persian (فارسی) from the list of languages on the left. Derive the nationality from the country name and write a sentence for each country/nationality.

6. In class, tell your classmates about friends with different nationalities than yours.

مثال: من دو دوست فِلِسطینی، یک دوست آمریکایی، سه دوست افغان و چند دوست اروپایی دارم.

7. Read the following words aloud with your partner. What do you notice about the relationship between the two words?

تاجیک: تاجیکِستان

تُرکَمَن: تُرکَمَنِستان

کُرد: کُردِستان

بَلوچ: بَلوچِستان

اُزبِک: اُزبِکِستان

هِندو: هِندوستان

8. Read the following words aloud with your partner. How does the suffix changes the meaning?

دانِش (knowledge): دانشگاه (university)

خواب (sleeping): خوابگاه (dorm)

فُروش (selling): فروشگاه (store)

فُرود (landing): فرودگاه (airport)

کار (work): کارگاه (workshop)

Listening Comprehension درک شنیدار

1. Watch the video and listen to what Shayli says. Follow the instructions.

....
....
....
....
....

PERSIAN OF IRAN TODAY

2. Listen to the audio file for the following words and write the sentences you hear for each item. Translate these sentences into English.

واژگان Vocabulary 3

ترجمه	نوشتار (گفتار)
Sangak bread	نانِ سنگک (نون سنگک)
my dear	عزیزم
bon appetit	نوش جان
It's me	من هستم (منم)
I come	می‌آیم (میام)
I am going	دارم می‌روم (دارم میرم)
Setar class	کلاسِ سه‌تار
ok	باشه
with, i.e., "with Leyli"	با : با لیلی
How is he/she?	چه طور است؟ (چه طوره؟)
How are you?	چه طور هستید؟ (چه طورین؟)
How is he / she / they?	چه طور هستند؟ (چه طورن؟)
my health, my state of being	حال من = حالم
God	خدا
thank God	خدا را شکر
you are welcome / go ahead (used to give permission)	اختیار دارید
Give my regards to…	به . . . سلام برسانید (برسونید)
of course, sure	حتماً
I'll give them your best.	(بزرگی‌تونو می‌رسونم)
my dear	جانم

Now watch the video and answer the following questions in Persian.

1. What did Raha ask her mother?
2. Where are Leili and Raha going?
3. What did Raha say to Mr. Ebadi as she was leaving?
4. Use the vocabulary you know to explain to a classmate what happened in the video.

Grammar Note — یادداشت دستوری

Find out for yourself!

Read the following words aloud with a partner. What is the relationship between the two columns?

Read the following words aloud with a partner. What is the relationship between the two columns?

کتاب‌ها	←	کتاب
میزها	←	میز
پدرها	←	پدر
صندلی‌ها	←	صندلی
مادرها	←	مادر
کامپیوترها	←	کامپیوتر
دفترها	←	دفتر

پرَستاران	←	پرَستار
مُهَندسان	←	مُهَندِس
مردان	←	مَرد
زَنان	←	زَن
مادَران	←	مادَر
برادَران	←	برادَر
پِدَران	←	پِدَر

Complete the following chart.

....	....	←	خواهر
....	....	←	شب
....	....	←	کیف
....	....	←	دختر

Write the rule for forming the plural below. What is the difference between the two different plurals above? Share your rule with your classmates and instructor, and refer to this page as a reference for the plural.

> ### Specific Direct Object Marker (را)

Read the following sentence:

این کتاب فارسی را باز کنید.

Try translating this sentence.

....

As you were translating, were there any words in the sentence you didn't understand?

....

You were able to translate the example sentence without knowing all of the words because را or *the specific direct object marker* is a concept that does not have an equivalent in English. Nevertheless, it is very important to Persian grammar. Our goal in this section is to familiarize you with the use of this word and the rules that govern it, so you can begin recognizing it and incorporating it into your own speaking and writing.

Basic Rules: Keep the following basic rules about را in mind as we introduce the concept to you in more detail.

> 1. را marks **specific** direct objects.
> 2. را is written immediately after the direct object or any adjectives that might describe it.
> 3. را is pronounced as though it were part of the word it follows. When you read aloud, for example, you cannot pause in between the direct object and را.
> 4. In spoken, را is pronounced as either /ro/ or /o/.

Direct Objects: Before we can explain را, it is important to review some of the basic grammar concepts that serve as a foundation for this feature. Specifically, it's important that we understand what a direct object is in English before we attempt to describe it in Persian.

A direct object is the thing or person upon which the verb's action is performed. Whereas the subject is the person or thing doing the action, the direct object is to whom or what that subject is performing the action. Consider the following sentence:

The teacher saw her before class.

The subject (the teacher) completed the action of the verb (seeing) upon her, so "her" is the direct object of this sentence.

Look at the following English sentences. Circle the direct object and explain how you determined it was the direct object. If there is no direct object, then simply explain why.

1. Every Tuesday I write a letter to my parents.

2. The carpenter built the chair from scratch.

3. The teacher slowly left the room on the last day of class.

4. Although both his parents are from Iran, he lives in the United States.

5. While he was in the classroom, he read a book.

As you might have noticed, whether or not a sentence has a direct object is determined by the verb. Some verbs like reading, writing, and building require an object, while other verbs like being, living, and going do not (because you don't perform those actions on anything). Verbs that take direct objects are called *transitive* and verbs that do not take direct objects are called *intransitive*.

Because the verb is an important (although not the only) factor in determining the use of را, it is important to categorize all of the verbs you learn as either *transitive* or *intransitive*. Keeping a list of transitive verbs will be very helpful to you as you attempt to master this concept.

بودن	آمدن	حرف زدن
باز کردن	زندگی کردن	داشتن
گوش کردن	حدس زدن	تکرار کردن
رفتن	کار کردن	دوست داشتن

For now, put the following verbs in the chart.

Intransitive	Transitive

Knowing whether or not the verb is transitive is the first step in determining whether or not to use را. If the verb is intransitive then you will never use را. Even though transitive verbs usually have direct objects, not all have direct objects.

Specificity: Once you have decided that a sentence has a direct object, you must determine whether or not this direct object is specific. Only **specific** direct objects require را. With regards to the direct object, specificity in Persian can function in two ways.

Sometimes the words that describe the direct object make it specific. In these cases it is grammatically incorrect to omit را. There are two cases when this is always true:
- Any time این and آن are the direct object or describe the direct object, you must use را. For example, can you translate the following sentences?

	این کتاب را دوست دارند.
	آن را تکرار کنید.

• Whenever a pronoun (or a pronominal ending) is the direct object or describes it, you must use را. Try translating the following sentences.

	ما را دوست دارند.
	دفترش را دارید.

2. Other times, by adding را after a direct object, you are making it specific. Consider these two examples:

I have books.	کتاب دارم.
I have the book. / I have that book.	آن کتاب را دارم. (کتابه رو دارم.)
We like ice cream.	بستنی دوست داریم.
We like the ice cream. / I like that ice cream.	آن بستنی را دوست داریم. (بستنیه رو دوست داریم.)

Can you explain what the presence of را does to each of these sentences? How does it change their meanings?

....
....

These are some basic rules to help you start determining specificity. However, ultimately a direct object is specific if both you and your listeners (or readers) know exactly what you're talking about. If it is a physical object, then they can picture it.

To Review:
1. را is written after specific direct objects.
2. Determining whether or not you need را involves a two-step thought process. First, you must decide if the verb is transitive and requires a direct object. Once you have decided that the sentence does have a direct object, you must determine whether or not the direct object is specific. Only specific direct objects require را. Can you describe how to decide if a direct object is specific?

....
....

Since this concept is completely new to you, it will take time to incorporate it comfortably into your speaking. Don't get discouraged! Instead, simply try to remain aware of this grammatical feature, making sure you understand it now and continue to review and update your understanding of it as we go along.

Grammar Practice 1

We will return to this concept several times over the next several months. For now, try writing five sentences that use را. Make sure that each sentence has at least six words and be prepared to explain in class why you used it.

۱. ....
۲. ....
۳. ....
۴. ....
۵. ....

Grammar Practice 2

Determine whether the following sentences need را. Remember your two-step thought process, looking first at the verb to see if it is transitive and then determining if the direct object is specific. Use the space to explain why you wrote را.

۱. شب به این خانه ــــ می‌رویم. ....
۲. آقا، آن جمله ــــ تکرار کنید. ....
۳. کتابم ــــ نداری؟ چرا آن ــــ دارم. ....
۴. به من ــــ گوش کنید! ....
۵. در آستین ــــ زندگی می‌کنیم. ....

در آمدی بر گذشته‌ی ساده — Introduction to Simple Past

This is an introduction to Simple Past in Persian. The following text is repeated in the second volume of the textbook. You will have the chance to learn and practice using the simple past tense in the next volume.

So far you have learned how to describe actions using the present tense. In Persian, the present tense is much more versatile than it is in English. We can use the present tense in Persian to refer to actions that are happening right now, will happen in the future, or happen habitually. However, we require several tenses to describe actions that take place in the past. The first past tense you will learn, the simple past, describes actions that were completed in the past but not over a period of time.

Examine the following example:

دیروز با دوستم چای خوردَم. (دیروز: yesterday)

1. Use the information you know in the sentence to try to translate it.

2. We will explain more clearly how to form the simple past below,

| I ate | خوردَم | to eat | خوردن |

177 PERSIAN OF IRAN TODAY

Forming the Simple Past

3. Look at the verb in the example sentence above. What is the infinitive for this verb?

Say the Persian infinitive "to eat" and then the conjugation "I ate." How do the two compare? What is the relationship between the infinitive and the conjugation?

The simple past tense in Persian follows this pattern:

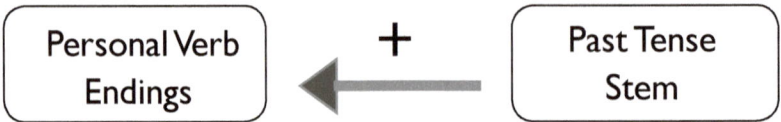

As you have probably already noticed, the past tense stem—unlike the present-tense stem—depends on the infinitive. In order to derive the past tense stem, we simply remove the ن from the infinitive.

The personal verb endings are the same endings we add to the present tense verb conjugations. The only exception is the third person singular (he/she/it); the past tense conjugation for this person is always just the past tense stem.

4. How would you translate this sentence into Persian?

Yesterday the professor had dinner with his mother.

5. Now that you have a basic understanding of the steps required to form the past tense conjugation, try filling in the chart. Read the conjugations aloud as you write them:

	من
	تو
خورد	او (اون)
	ما
خوردید (خوردین)	شما
	آنها (اونا)

Speaking Activities حرف زدن

In Class:
Watch Video 10 with your instructor and learn more about meeting and greeting others. Practice these new expressions with your classmates. Ask them where they are from and tell them where you are from. You'll certainly want to let them know that you are pleaesd to meet them!

For Homework:

Carefully review the new classroom vocabulary (pg. 169). Listen to the audio file so you will recognize these words and expressions when you hear them. Your teacher will be using these phrases often and you will need to use them to function in class. Try to use this vocabulary as much as possible when you speak to your teachers and classmates.

Memorize the following sentence and use it when you are saying goodbye to someone you have just met for the first time. !خیلی خوشوقت شدم

Language Games

1. Flashcard Game
Bring your vocabulary flashcards to class for this flashcard activity.

Trade flashcards with a partner. Come up with questions for each word you encounter on your partner's flashcards. Your partner must answer these questions. Then switch roles.

2. Sentence Master
The class will be given five words. Each group should try to write 5 sentences. In each sentence they will use as many words as they can. The number of the words used by each group to write the sentences will be the score for each group. Prepositions and connectors will not count.

Write your sentences on the board. You will have an opportunity to correct your sentences as you write them. However, once you are done the other groups may identify any mistakes in your sentences, and each mistake will cause you to lose a point. Keep spelling, punctuation, word order, and the proper prepositions in mind!

Classroom Activities — فعالیت‌های پیشنهادی

Talk with your classmates and find out...

    ...if their studies are hard or easy.

    ... how many close friends they have.

    ... what is next to your house.

    ... now how many chairs there are in the class.

    ... where they were yesterday at 12:45.

    ... what they do between 8:30 in the morning and 8:30 at night.

    ... if they talk on the phone everyday.

    ... if they like reading.

Review Exercises

دوره واژگان و دستور

Spelling:

این بخش برای دانشجویان ایرانی- آمریکایی است که معنی واژه‌ها را می‌دانند.

1. Have someone read the following words and sentences to you and try to write them down.

Unit 1 and 2:

ننیس، زیاد، سینا، ندوز، دیس، امیر، ساناز، پارسا، شینا، پاییز، آنیتا، بیتا، آستین، ایران، تبریز، پریا
اتریش، اندونزی، پاناما، روسیه، سوریه، ارمنستان، اسپانیا، پاریس، اتیوپی، رشت، شیراز، تنسی

سینا نان بربری دوست دارد.
سیب را بردار.
دیروز بارانی بود.
دندان درد دارید؟
ایران در آسیاست.
او نسرین است یا نسترن؟
او دو روز در زندان بود.
این رستوران سوپ سبزی دارد.
درز آستینت را بدوز.
تو را برای دیدن پدرت برد؟

برای شام پیتزا و سیب‌زمینی داشتیم.
سه روز است نمی‌توانم دستم را پایین بیاورم.
تمام روز شاد بودم.
پیتات یا بادام زمینی؟
دوست تنیس‌بازم در اتریش می‌ماند.
اسمش را نمی‌دانم.
پسر برادرم از مار می‌ترسد.
این بازی من را می‌ترساند.
درس سه درس آسانی بود.
به او آب دادم.

Unit 3 and 4:

بیشتر مردم ایران مسلمان هستند.
تمام دانشجویان بیرون نشسته بودند.
همدان شهر مادرم است. پدرم مشهدی است.
آن پسر ایرانی در مجارستان به مدرسه می‌رود.
او را در ویرجینیا دیدم.
تهرانی‌ها هوای سالم ندارند.
آب هویج بستنی یک نوشیدنی ایرانی است.
اینجا بهترین بستنی شهر را دارد.
پنجره‌ی اینجا همیشه بسته است.
آلمان پناهجویان را راه داد.
خواهر و برادرم سوپ جو دوست دارند.
خوش آمدید! تشریف بیارید تو!

Short form of "to be"

2. Use contractions to change the following sentences? (In other words, how else can we say the following sentences?)

۱. مادر من معلم است.

۲. ما دانشجو هستیم.

۳. دوستان ما عصبانی هستند.

۴. پدر و مادر شما اهل ایران نیستند؟

Ezâfe

3. Add *ezâfe* wherever necessary.

۱. در یک رستوران بزرگ کار می‌کنیم.

۲. مادر و خواهرش پنجاه تا کیف زیبا دارند.

۳. چند نفر در این آپارتمان قشنگ و زیبا زندگی می‌کنند؟

۴. خانه شما چند در دارد؟ پنجره بزرگ هم دارد؟

4. Add the *ezâfe* marker and then translate to English.

۱. یک میز بزرگ در خانه‌مان داریم. ....

۲. قهوه گرمم را در کافی شاپ دانشگاه‌مان نمی‌خورم. ....

۳. ساعت پنج عصر به کلاس فیزیک می‌روم. ....

۴. آمنه یک کیف بزرگ و دو خودکار کوچک دارد. ....

۵. من و دوست ایرانی‌ام به رستوران اصفهان می‌رویم. ....

Vocabulary

5. Complete the following sentences.

۱. - .... به خانه می‌روی؟ - ساعت دو

گفتاری: (- .... می‌ری خونه؟ - ساعت دو)

۲. .... ؟ . بد نیستم.

۳. صندلی .... ؟ . کنار میز است.

۴. پدرتان .... ؟ . مهندس است.

۵. .... ؟ . نه، زیر دفترم است.

۶. .... ؟ . نمی‌دانم کجاست.

۷. .... ؟ . نه، ناراحت هستم. امتحان داریم.

Writing questions

6. Write a question for each sentence. Make sure that the question is related to the underlined section.

۱. پدر و مادرشان <u>به رستوران</u> می‌روند. ....

۲. <u>در کویت</u> زندگی می‌کنم. ....

۳. <u>۰۹۱۷-۸۷۹-۲۱۲۳</u> ....

۴. <u>او و دوستش</u> به خانه‌ی مادرم می‌روند. ....

۵. آنها <u>در یک رستوران ژاپنی</u> چای می‌خورند. ....

Verbs and pronouns

7. Complete the chart.

ضمیر فاعلی	حال ساده رفتن	ضمیر ملکی	حال ساده آمدن
من	می‌روم (می‌رم)		می‌آیم (می‌آم)
تو			
او			
ما			
شما			
آنها		خواهرشان (خواهرِشون)	

8. Use the approriate forms of to be, to eat, to live, to like, to go and to have to complete the following sentences.

۱. من و مریم در خیابان نادی ....

۲. این چهار زن به دانشگاه قطر ....

۳. شما و دوستاتان جمعه به خانه‌ی ما ....

۴. من در اتاقم چهار صندلی و سه میز ....

۵. آن زن جوان پپسی ....

۶. شما اهل کجا .... ؟

Word order

Persian syntax is quite ambiguous in written form. Several factors contribute to the ambiguity: Although Persian is a verb-final language, it does not adhere to a strict word order and the sentential constituents may occur in various positions in the clause; this is especially the case for preposition phrases and adverbials. In addition, there are no overt markers, such as case morphology, to indicate the function of a noun phrase or its boundary; in Persian, only specific direct objects receive an overt marker. Although in spoken language, the ezafe morpheme is used to link the elements within the noun phrase, this morpheme, being a short vowel, is absent in written text. Furthermore, subjects are optional in Persian and subject-verb agreement is not always present for inanimate subjects. Persian preposition phrases, however, are easily recognized and can be used to mark phrasal boundaries in the sentence. Additionally, the verb almost always occurs in the sentence-final position in written text. For more information, you can check: http://www.zoorna.org/shiraz/syntax.html

9. Put in order. Do not forget the punctuation.

۱. هستند، شما، پدر، کجا ....

۲. خانم، در، هجده، هستند، کلاس، آن ....

۳. شیر، آن، زیبا، نمی‌خورد، دختر ....

۴. دوست، چند، دانشگاه، می‌رود، ساعت، به، اتان ....

۵. وانیلی، میل، بستنی، دارید ....

۶. گرم، شیر، می‌خوری، چند، ساعت ....

۷. بزرگ، صندلی، هستند، پانزده، آن ....

۸. رستوران، چند، این، در، است، میز ....

۹. دوستم، کویت، کشور، در، برادر، زندگی می‌کند ....

۱۰. هر روز، درس، چند، می‌خواند، می‌دانی، ساعت ؟ ....

۱۱. ژاپن، امّا، اهل، ژاپنی، نیستند، حرف می‌زنند، آنها ....

۱۲. می‌دانی، کیف، زیر، کجا، است، میز، شان، نیست (۲ جمله) ....

۱۳. هستند، پدر، مادر، چه، و، اش، کاره؟ ....

۱۴. سوال، جواب، نمی‌دانم، تان، را ....

۱۵. عصبانی، چون، آنها، دوست، غذا، شان، هستند، نمی‌خورد ....

۱۶. داری، فیزیک، ساعت، کلاس، می‌دانی، چند ....

۱۷. کجا، است، فیزیک، کلاس، َت ....

۱۸. نیست، دانشگاه، در، شما، انقلاب، خیابان ....

۱۹. یک، آمریکایی، بزرگ، دانشگاه، خانه، پشت، ام، است ....

۲۰. را، مرد، عصبانی، غذا، اش/ایش، و، ناراحت، نمی‌خورد ....

۲۱. می‌روم، صد، پنجاه، و، شهر، ایران، به ....

۲۲. روی، نیست، میز، کجا، قهوه، نمی‌دانم، اتان، است ....

۲۳. خیابان، رستوران، در، دارند، هشت، این، آنها، است، و، ژاپنی، سوشی ....

۲۴. روی، خانه، است، میز، اتان، بزرگم، کیف ....

۲۵. کجا، آنها، بچّه، نمی‌دانم، کوچک، است ....

۲۶. خانه، مان، بزرگ، صندلی، داریم، ما، میز، زیبا، چهار، در، دو، و ....

۲۷. دوستم، می‌روم، خانه، به، ساعت، سوپرمارکت، پنج، غذا، در، می‌خوریم، و ....

10. Use fifteen of the following words to write a conversation.

زندگی می‌کنند، پنجره، خواهر، نیستم، دفتر، جوان، نمی‌دانم، صندلی، اهل، هفت، امّا، خوشحال، خسته، آب، سرد، می‌خورید، تشنه، نیستند اینجا، شهر

11. Use the following words to write a conversation.

پشت، معلّم، نفر، ساعت چند؟، ناهار، گرسنه، هشتاد، دفتر، با اجازه‌ی شما، کجا

گفت‌وگوهای کوتاه درس اول — Short Conversations Unit 1

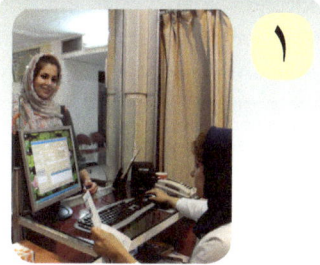

۱
- اسم شما چیه؟
- اسم من سمانه است.

۲
- حال شما چه طوره؟
- خوبم، متشکرم. شما چه طورین؟
- خوبم، خیلی ممنون.

۳
- سلام، صبح به خیر!
- صبح به خیر.

گفت‌وگوهای کوتاه درس دوم — Short Conversations Unit 2

۱
- خیلی ممنون!
- خواهش می‌کنم.

۲
- ببخشید!
- خواهش می‌کنم.

۳
- بفرمایید.
- خیلی ممنون!
- خواهش می‌کنم.

۴
- حالت چه‌طوره؟
- خوبم. تو چه‌طوری؟
- منم خوبم. متشکّرم.

۵
- حالتون چه‌طوره؟
- خوبم، مرسی. شما چه‌طورین؟
- بد نیستم. خدا را شکر.

185 PERSIAN OF IRAN TODAY

فهرست واژگان درس‌ها

kitchen	آشپزخانه (آشپزخونه)	۲۶		opera	اپرا	۱
sir, gentleman, man	آقا	۲۷		room	اتاق	۲
United States	آمریکا	۲۸		bedroom	اتاق خواب	۳
American	آمریکایی	۲۹		guest room	اتاق مهمان	۴
to come, I come	آمدن، می‌آیم	۳۰		you are welcome / go ahead (used to give permission)	اختیار دارید	۵
that	آن (اون)	۳۱		is	است	۶
it, that	آن (اون)	۳۲		professor	استاد	۷
there	آنجا (اونجا)	۳۳		ski	اسکی	۸
they	آنها (اونا)	۳۴		name	اسم	۹
with	با	۳۵		now	الان	۱۰
with your permission	با اجازه‌ی شما	۳۶		but	امّا	۱۱
with, i.e., "with Leyli"	با: با لیلی	۳۷		pomegranate	انار	۱۲
almond	بادام	۳۸		English	انگلیسی	۱۳
open	باز کُنید (باز کنین)	۳۹		to be from somewhere	اهلِ	۱۴
ok	باشه	۴۰		he, she	او (اون)	۱۵
over/above	بالا	۴۱		Iranian	ایرانی	۱۶
close	بَبندید (ببندین)	۴۲		he, she (polite)	ایشان (ایشون)	۱۷
excuse me	ببخشید	۴۳		this	این	۱۸
child	بچّه، کودَک	۴۴		it's warm in here, it's warm, I'm hot	اینجا گرمه، گرمه، گرممه	۱۹
read	بخوانید (بخونین)	۴۵		here	اینجا/ این‌جا	۲۰
bad	بد	۴۶		Iran	ایران	۲۱
brother	برادَر	۴۷		this	این	۲۲
big	بزُرگ	۴۸		water	آب	۲۳
I'll give them your best.	بزرگی‌تونو می‌رسونه	۴۹		fruit juice	آب‌میوه	۲۴
ice cream	بستَنی	۵۰		easy	آسان (آسون)	۲۵
I know (how to do something), you know	بَلَدم، بَلَدی	۵۱				

فهرست واژگان درس‌ها

behind	پشت	۷۹	yes	بله	۵۲
stairs	پله	۸۰	write	بنویسید (بنویسین)	۵۳
five	پنج	۸۱	to	به	۵۴
window	پنجره/ پنجَره	۸۲	Give my regards to…	به … سلام برسانید (برسونید)	۵۵
fifty	پنجاه	۸۳	I go to	به … می‌رَوَم (می‌رم)	۵۶
cheese	پنیر	۸۴	I was	بودم	۵۷
old	پیر	۸۵	twenty	بیست	۵۸
Quantifier	تا	۸۶	He is twenty years old.	بیست سالشه- بیست سال دارد	۵۹
thirsty	تشنه	۸۷	I am twenty.	بیست سالمه- بیست سال دارم.	۶۰
I am thirsty.	تشنه‌ام (تشنَمه)	۸۸	twenty six	بیست و شش	۶۱
repeat	تکرار کُنید (تکرار کنین)	۸۹	twenty five	بیست و پنج	۶۲
television	تلویزیون	۹۰	twenty four	بیست و چهار	۶۳
exercise	تمرین	۹۱	twenty two	بیست و دو	۶۴
lazy	تنبل	۹۲	twenty three	بیست و سه	۶۵
tennis	تنیس	۹۳	twenty nine	بیست و نه	۶۶
Tehran / from Tehran	تهران/ تهرانی	۹۴	twenty eight	بیست و هشت	۶۷
you	تو	۹۵	twenty seven	بیست و هفت	۶۸
my dear	جانم	۹۶	twenty one	بیست و یک	۶۹
in front of	جلو	۹۷	twenty / thirty	بیست، سی	۷۰
sentence	جمله	۹۸	between	بین	۷۱
answer	جواب	۹۹	park	پارک	۷۲
young	جوان	۱۰۰	eraser	پاک‌کن	۷۳
tea	چای	۱۰۱	fifteen	پانزدَه (پونزده)	۷۴
how many	چند (چند تا)	۱۰۲	father	پدَر	۷۵
how old are you?	چند سالتونه؟- چند سال دارید؟	۱۰۳	my father	پدرم	۷۶
how many?	چند؟	۱۰۴	nurse	پرستار	۷۷
			boy, son	پسَر	۷۸

فهرست واژگان درس‌ها

forty	چِهِل	۱۰۵	thank God	خدا را شکر	۱۲۹
what	چه (چی)	۱۰۶	tired	خسته	۱۳۰
How is he/she?	چه طور است؟ (چه طوره؟)	۱۰۷	dormitory	خوابگاه	۱۳۱
How is he / she / they?	چه طور هستند؟ (چه طورن؟)	۱۰۸	sister/ my sister	خواهَر/خواهرم	۱۳۲
How are you?	چه طور هستید؟ (چه طورین؟)	۱۰۹	you're welcome	خواهش می‌کُنَم	۱۳۳
What are you doing?	چه کار می‌کُنید؟	۱۱۰	good	خوب	۱۳۴
what does he do? What do they do?	چه کاره هستند؟	۱۱۱	pen	خودکار	۱۳۵
what do you do?	چه کاره هستید؟	۱۱۲	handsome	خوش تیپ	۱۳۶
who	چه کسی/ (کی؟)	۱۱۳	happy	خوش‌حال	۱۳۷
what?	چه/ چه چیزی/ (چی؟)	۱۱۴	street	خیابان (خیابون)	۱۳۸
four	چهار (چاهار)	۱۱۵	thank you	خیلی مَمنون	۱۳۹
fourteen	چهاردَه (چارده)	۱۱۶	welcome!	خیلی خوش آمدید!	۱۴۰
because	چون	۱۱۷	he / she has	دارَد	۱۴۱
how are you?	حال شما چه طور است؟ (... چه طوره؟)	۱۱۸	I have / I do not have	دارَم/ نَدارَم	۱۴۲
my health, my state of being	حال من = حالم	۱۱۹	he / she has, they have	دارَند	۱۴۳
of course, sure	حتماً	۱۲۰	you have (for close friends)	داری	۱۴۴
guess	حدس بزَنید (حدس بزنین)	۱۲۱	I am going	دارم می‌روم (دارم میرم)	۱۴۵
speak	حرف بزَنید (حرف بزنین)	۱۲۲	you have / you do not have	دارید/ نَدارید	۱۴۶
ma'am, lady, Mrs., Miss	خانُم	۱۲۳	we have	داریم	۱۴۷
house	خانه (خونه)	۱۲۴	student (non-university)	دانش‌آموز/ شاگرد	۱۴۸
your house	خانه‌اتان (خونه‌تون)	۱۲۵	university student	دانِشجو	۱۴۹
house wife	خانه‌دار	۱۲۶	university	دانشگاه	۱۵۰
your house	خانه‌ی شما	۱۲۷	girl, daughter	دخترَ	۱۵۱
God	خدا	۱۲۸	door	در	۱۵۲
			in	در (تو)	۱۵۳
			lesson	درس	۱۵۴
			restroom	دستشویی	۱۵۵

فهرست واژگان درس‌ها

۱۵۶	دفتر	notebook		۱۸۵	سؤال	question
۱۵۷	دکتر	doctor		۱۸۶	سوپ	soup
۱۵۸	ده	ten		۱۸۷	سوپر مارکت	super market
۱۵۹	دو	two		۱۸۸	سی	thirty
۱۶۰	دوازده	twelve		۱۸۹	سیب	apple
۱۶۱	دوست دارم	I like		۱۹۰	سیزده	thirteen
۱۶۲	دوست دارید	you like		۱۹۱	سینما	movie theater
۱۶۳	دوست ندارم	I do not like		۱۹۲	شام	dinner
۱۶۴	دوست ندارید	you do not like		۱۹۳	شانزده (شونزده)	sixteen
۱۶۵	دوست/دوستم	friend / my friend		۱۹۴	شب به خیر	good night. (when you are going to bed at night)
۱۶۶	رستوران	restaurant		۱۹۵	شش (شیش)	six
۱۶۷	رادیو	radio		۱۹۶	شصت	sixty
۱۶۸	راهرو	hallway		۱۹۷	شغل	occupation
۱۶۹	رشته	major		۱۹۸	شغل شما چیست؟ (شغلِ شما چیه؟)	what is your job?
۱۷۰	رو، روی	on		۱۹۹	شما	you (plural or respectful singular)
۱۷۱	روز به خیر	good morning/day		۲۰۰	شیرینی	sweets, dessert
۱۷۲	روزنامه‌نگار/ خبرنگار	journalist		۲۰۱	صبح به خیر	good morning.
۱۷۳	زن	woman		۲۰۲	صبح/ صبحانه	morning / breakfast
۱۷۴	زندگی می‌کنم	I live		۲۰۳	صد/ هزار	a hundred/a thousand
۱۷۵	زیبا	beautiful		۲۰۴	صندلی	chair
۱۷۶	زیر	under		۲۰۵	ظهر به خیر	greeting for noon
۱۷۷	ژاکت	jacket		۲۰۶	عالی	excellent
۱۷۸	ساعتِ دو	two o'clock		۲۰۷	عبارت	term, phrase
۱۷۹	ساعتِ یک	one o'clock		۲۰۸	عراق	Iraq
۱۸۰	ساعت چند؟/ کِی	what time? when?		۲۰۹	عربستان سعودی	Saudi Arabia
۱۸۱	سخت	hard, difficult		۲۱۰	عزیزم	my dear
۱۸۲	سرد/ (سَردَمه)	cold/ I'm cold, It's cold		۲۱۱	عصبانی	angry
۱۸۳	سلام	hello				
۱۸۴	سه	three				

189 PERSIAN OF IRAN TODAY

فهرست واژگان درس‌ها

teacher	مُعَلِّم	۲۴۰		good afternoon.	عصر به خیر	۲۱۲
I	من	۲۴۱		I eat food. (never use khordan by itself)	غذا می‌خورم	۲۱۳
I am	من هستم (منم)	۲۴۲		Persian	فارسی	۲۱۴
It's me	مُهَندِس	۲۴۳		soccer	فوتبال	۲۱۵
engineer	می‌آیم (میام)	۲۴۴		coffee	قهوه	۲۱۶
I come	می‌خُورم	۲۴۵		I work	کار می‌کُنَم	۲۱۷
I eat, I drink	می‌خُورید؟ (می‌خورین)	۲۴۶		kabob	کباب	۲۱۸
do you eat/drink?	میز	۲۴۷		book	کتاب	۲۱۹
table	میل دارید؟ (میل دارین)	۲۴۸		library	کتاب‌خانه	۲۲۰
would you like (to have)?	میوه	۲۴۹		where-where is it?	کجا، کجاست	۲۲۱
fruit	می‌خوریم	۲۵۰		word	کَلَمه، واژه	۲۲۲
we eat, we drink	می‌دانم (می‌دونم)	۲۵۱		class	کلاس	۲۲۳
I know (knowledge)	می‌دانی (می‌دونی)	۲۵۲		Setar class	کلاسِ سه‌تار	۲۲۴
you know	ناراحَت	۲۵۳		beside	کنار	۲۲۵
sad	نان سنگک (نون سنگک)	۲۵۴		concert	کنسرت	۲۲۶
Sangak bread	نان (نون)	۲۵۵		small	کوچَک (کوچیک)	۲۲۷
bread	ناهار / نهار	۲۵۶		bag	کیف	۲۲۸
lunch	نبودم	۲۵۷		I am hungry.	گرسنه‌ام (گُرسَنَمه)	۲۲۹
I was not	نزدیک	۲۵۸		to say, I say	گفتن، می‌گویم	۲۳۰
close	نَفَر	۲۵۹		listen, listen to	گوش کُنید. به ... گوش کنید (گوش کنین)	۲۳۱
Quantifier for person	نمی‌دانم (نمی‌دونم)	۲۶۰		we	ما	۲۳۲
I do not know.	نه	۲۶۱		mother	مادَر	۲۳۳
nine	نه	۲۶۲		my mother	مادرم	۲۳۴
no	نَوَد	۲۶۳		marker	ماژیک	۲۳۵
ninety	نوزَده	۲۶۴		thank you	متشکّرم	۲۳۶
nineteen	نوش جان	۲۶۵		pencil	مداد	۲۳۷
bon appetit	نوشابه	۲۶۶		man	مرد	۲۳۸
I am not	نیستَم	۲۶۷		sick	مریض	۲۳۹

فهرست واژگان درس‌ها

۲۶۸	نیستید (نیستین)	you are not
۲۶۹	نیستیم	we are not
۲۷۰	هال/ اتاق نشیمن	living room
۲۷۱	هجدَه (هیژده)	eighteen
۲۷۲	هستَم	I am
۲۷۳	هستَند	they are
۲۷۴	هستی	you are
۲۷۵	هستید (هستین)	you are
۲۷۶	هستیم	we are
۲۷۷	هشت	eight
۲۷۸	هشتاد	eighty
۲۷۹	هفت	seven
۲۸۰	هفتاد	seventy
۲۸۱	هفدَه (هیوده)	seventeen
۲۸۲	و	and
۲۸۳	ورزِش	sport, exercise
۲۸۴	وکیل	lawyer
۲۸۵	ویلا	villa
۲۸۶	یک	one
۲۸۷	یا	or
۲۸۸	یازدَه	eleven